TOMOSHIBI

The colour of the cloth cover is that of the official dress of the Crown Prince. It was chosen since the original Japanese edition of Tomoshibi *was published when Their Imperial Majesties were still the Crown Prince and Princess. The pictures on the preceding pages show the Emperor and Empress in formal court attire.*

Tomoshibi

Light

Collected Poetry by Emperor Akihito
and Empress Michiko

edited by Marie Philomène *and* Masako Saito

New York • WEATHERHILL • *Tokyo*

The calligraphy for *Tomoshibi* on the cover
was written by Chikkei Miyamoto.

First edition, 1991

Published by Weatherhill, Inc., New York, with editorial offices at
Tanko-Weatherhill, Inc., 8-3 Nibancho, Chiyoda-ku, Tokyo 102,
Japan. Copyright © 1991 by the Board of the Chamberlains, Im-
perial Household Agency; all rights reserved. Printed and first
published in Japan.

Library of Congress Cataloging-in-Publication Data: Akihito, Emperor of
Japan, 1933– / [Tomoshibi. English & Japanese] / Tomoshibi = Light:
collected poetry / by the Emperor Akihito and the Empress Michiko;
edited by Marie Philomène and Masako Saito.—1st ed. / p.   cm. /
Translation of: Tomoshibi. / ISBN 0-8348-0237-6 / 1. Waka—Trans-
lations into English. 2. Waka, English—Translations from Japa-
nese. I. Michiko, Empress, consort of Akihito, Emperor of Japan,
1934– . II. De los Reyes, Marie Philomène, 1919–   . III.
Saitō, Masako, 1931– . IV. Title. V. Title: Light. / PL845.K456T66
1990 / 895.6′15—dc20 / CIP 90-21979

Contents

Introduction

On the occasion of the enthronement of Emperor Akihito and Empress Michiko, it seems timely to publish their joint collection of *waka* poems, *Tomoshibi*, in a language that can be read by people of many nations. These poems were written and first published in Japanese when the Emperor and Empress were Crown Prince and Princess. With this fact in mind, the reader will be better able to appreciate both the subject matter and the style of language used in several of the poems.

The Japanese tradition of writing poetry can be traced back to the 8th-century *Manyōshū*, the *Collection of Ten Thousand Leaves*. Since that time, members of the nobility have made every effort to excel in the writing of waka. As Robert Huey tells us in his volume *Kyogoku Tamekane, Poetry and Politics in Late Kamakura Japan*, it was the practice at the time for aristocratic courtier-politicians, emperors, crown princes, and even retired emperors to devote considerable time to encouraging popular participation in the numerous poetry contests which they regularly organized.

However, it was not until 1869, at the beginning of the Meiji era, that the Emperor established the New Year's Poetry Reading as an annual event at the Imperial Court. These gatherings, for which poems were specially contributed, soon developed into courtly ceremonies. Then, beginning in 1874, ordinary citizens were encouraged to submit their poetic compositions at New Year and the event became so popular that, starting in 1879, the best of the poems submitted by citizens were read before the Emperor and, from 1882, were published. But it is only since 1950 that those citizens who have written winning poems have been invited to attend the New Year's Poetry Readings.

A word of explanation should, perhaps, be given now of the term waka. Literally meaning Japanese songs, it came to denote Japanese lyric forms in the days before the Imperial Court was moved from Kyoto in 1868, and includes the *chōka, tanka* and *sedōka* poetic forms.

The longer chōka comprises a number of five-syllable and seven-syllable couplets and ends with a seven-syllable line to which one or more envoys, or *hanka*, may be attached. The tanka is a shorter poem, consisting of 31 syllables grouped in five lines, of which the first and third contain five syllables and the others seven. The sedōka comprises two three-line stanzas, each with five, seven, and seven syllables, respectively.

Of the above three forms, the tanka is considered the norm of Japanese poetry, so much so that today, when one speaks of waka, one is usually referring to tanka.

Aside from the poems chanted at the New Year's Poetry Reading at the Imperial Court, waka written by some 50 people including members of the Imperial Family and their relatives are submitted to the Emperor on a fixed day of the month, the theme for each month being decided in advance. The poems are then printed and distributed to their authors. Many of the poems in *Tomoshibi* were written for such occasions, while others commemorate events attended by the Emperor and Empress when they were Crown Prince and Princess, or record their recollections of people. Of the 166 poems penned by the Emperor, 160 are waka and six are *ryūka*. The ryūka, consisting of three eight-syllable lines followed by a final six-syllable line, was developed

8

in the kingdom of Ryūkyū and written in its language. Of the 140 waka by the Empress, one is a chōka (No. 96) and the rest are tanka.

While the writing of waka by the Emperor and Empress follows Imperial Family tradition, this is the first time that a joint collection of Imperial waka has been published in English. To commemorate the 70th anniversary of the 1912 demise of Emperor Meiji, two booklets were published: one in 1982, containing waka of Emperor Meiji, and the other in 1984, with waka written by Empress Shoken. But no English publication followed, although each booklet did include an English translation of the verses. This is also true in the case of *Akebono*, a collection of waka by Emperor Showa and Empress Nagako.

The editors decided that although the English translation of the *Tomoshibi* waka should respect the five-line pattern, it could deviate from the traditional waka pattern of five-seven-five-seven-seven syllables so as to allow concentration on grasping the imagery and atmosphere of the works.

The editors and collaborators wish to express their gratitude to Their Majesties for having given so much of their time to provide the information necessary to clarify the meaning of compositions. Furthermore, gratitude is due to Her Majesty who allowed some of her own translations to be published, as indicated in the notes. To the consultants, Professor Rikutaro Fukuda, Dr. Peter Milward and Mrs. Kristen Deming, we extend our gratitude for generous advice.

It is our hope that this English translation may lead to a better understanding of the Emperor and Empress, as also of Japan and its people. For it is their cultural traditions that, reflected in the literary activities of the Imperial Family, reveal Japan as a land where beauty of spirit is expressed in song.

Marie Philomène de los Reyes

9

EMPEROR AKIHITO

1945

At Lake Yu

The mountain ash
Has turned red
By the roadside.
Autumn has certainly arrived
At the shore of Lake Yu.   *(1)*

Unawares
The larch leaves
Have turned yellow.
So softly on them
The rain is falling.   *(2)*

At the Akasaka Detached Palace

When do the crows in flocks
Finally sleep?
They are still
Swarming in the sky,
Though the night has come.   *(3)*

1 Lake Yu: during World War II, Emperor Akihito was for a while evacuated
to Nikkō, Tochigi Prefecture. The lake is in the northwest of the city,
1,478 metres above sea level.

1947

At Yakushiji

Verdant is the wood
Of Yakushiji,
Wherein towers
The three-storied pagoda,
Its vermilion now faded.   *(4)*

At Ishiyamadera

On the waters
Of Lake Biwa
The rain falls,
Faintly veiling
Seta no Karahashi.   *(5)*

4, 5 Visiting Kansai, the region incorporating Kyoto, Osaka and surrounding
prefectures.
4 Yakushiji: one of the three main temples of the Hossō sect of Buddhism, it
was built at its present location in a suburb of Nara City mostly during the
720s.
5 Ishiyamadera: located in Ōtsu City, Shiga Prefecture, it is a ranking temple of
the Shingon sect of Buddhism and is said to have been founded in 749.
   Lake Biwa: located in Shiga Prefecture, it is Japan's largest freshwater lake,
with an area of 673.8 square kilometres.
   Seta no Karahashi: literally the 'Chinese-style bridge of Seta', it is a bridge
spanning the Seta River which flows south from Lake Biwa.

Fireflies over the Paddy Fields

> A gentle night breeze
> Blows over the paddy fields
> And flitting fireflies,
> Mirrored in the water,
> Become twinkling stars.   *(6)*

1948

Near Kisarazu

> On a spring day
> In fields mown after the harvest,
> The surface of thin ice
> Sheathing bubbles inside
> Glitters white in the sun.   *(7)*

> On a boat left
> In the tideland,
> Branches of pine and bamboo
> Have been set up
> To celebrate the New Year.   *(8)*

---

6 Title: theme for the birthday of Empress Teimei (1884–1951), grandmother
of Emperor Akihito.
7–9 Visiting Chiba Prefecture.
7, 8 Kisarazu: a city in Chiba Prefecture, on Tokyo Bay.

Near Tomisaki

The wind storming
Over the ocean,
The white-crested waves
Break on rocks
And blow up foaming spray.　　(9)

Nachi Falls

Whence do these petals
Come drifting,
I wonder!
Carried by the wind,
They are crossing the valley.　　(10)

9 Tomisaki: a Pacific coast locality in Tateyama City, southern Chiba Pre-
fecture.
10, 11 Visiting Kishū, formerly a province comprising the present Wakayama
Prefecture and part of Mie Prefecture.
10 Nachi Falls: the falls, 133 metres high, is on the upper reaches of the
Nachi River, southeastern Wakayama Prefecture.

A View over Kushimoto

Looking down over
The blue inlet
Of Kushimoto,
I see wave upon white wave
Advancing in rows.   *(11)*

1949

At Numazu

Disturbing for a moment
The calm surface
Of the sea,
A school of fish comes
Rushing in, raising ripples.   *(12)*

11 Kushimoto: a town in southern Wakayama Prefecture, on the Pacific coast.
12 Numazu: a city on Suruga Bay, eastern Shizuoka Prefecture.

1950

Clear Water of a Pond

The pond's surface
Is covered with cherry blossoms.
From the water,
Clear to the depths, rises
The atmosphere of springtime.   *(13)*

The Capital in Fresh Verdure

The morning sunlight
Brightens the rows of trees
Fresh in their verdure
By the roadsides
Of the capital.   *(14)*

---

13 Title: theme for the birthday of Emperor Showa (1901–89), the father of
Emperor Akihito.
14 Title: theme for the wedding of Princess Kazuko (1925–89), an elder sister
of Emperor Akihito.

1951

On the Demise of Empress Teimei

> Whereas trees and grass
> In the garden
> Are green,
> Not a sound is heard on the stairway
> Of the Empress Dowager's Palace. *(15)*

> Once more
> If only I could see
> My grandmother!
> I have not yet told her
> About the horse show. *(16)*

Garden Plot in Summer

> On a summer day
> Green is the garden plot
> In the palace;
> Yet, who would find joy in it
> Since my grandmother has
>   passed away? *(17)*

15, 16 Empress Teimei: see Emperor's poem 6.
17 Title: theme for the mourning for Empress Teimei.

1953

Departing Ship

> Departing by ship
> I will cross
> Rough seas
> To travel far and wide
> And see what foreign lands are like.

(18)

In Edinburgh

> On the surface
> Of the deserted lake,
> A swan was alone.
> As I lingered there,
> It drew near to me.

(19)

18 Title: theme for the New Year's Poetry Reading.
19–32 On a trip to attend the coronation of H.M. Queen Elizabeth II and
the succeeding tour of Europe and the United States of America.

In Scotland

Driving
Over the moors
Thick with heather,
We head for the castle
Of the Duke of Buccleuch.   (*20*)

Upon a hill
Strewn with rocks and
Dark brown heather,
Black-faced sheep
Ramble in flocks.   (*21*)

The Farne Islands

The lighthouse
Whose tale I was told
In my childhood days,
I now approach in a boat
Over the waves.   (*22*)

22, 23 Farne Islands: a group of seventeen small islands, now a bird sanctuary,
off the northeast coast of Northumberland, northern England. The lighthouse
on Longstone was the home of Grace Darling, famous for her part in rescu-
ing survivors from the wrecked Forfarshire in 1838.

Among clumps of grass
Wild ducks resting,
Brood on their eggs
And do not move
When men come close.   (23)

Eve of the Coronation

Walking
In the city late at night,
I see pavements
Crowded with people
Who will spend all night there.   (24)

In Spain

Outside the town,
We drive a car,
Passing hill after hill
Dappled with grass
Under the strong sun.   (25)

24 Coronation: the coronation of H.M. Queen Elizabeth II took place at
Westminster Abbey on June 2.

At the Palace of Laeken, Belgium

> The car which
> The young King drives
> Through woods
> Speckled with sunlight
> Hastens to the horse-riding ground.   *(26)*

In Germany

> Fascinated
> By the scenery
> Of woods and fields,
> On the autobahn I have been
> Unaware of the passing of time.   *(27)*

In Norway

> Pervaded by mist
> As far as the eye can see,
> Extends a plateau
> Where no tree grows,
> Strewn with many stones.   *(28)*

---

26 Young King: H.M. Baudouin I became king of the Belgians in 1951, at the age of twenty.

In Wyoming

We have driven
Miles, and yet
Unchanged is the landscape
Extending before us—
A wasteland devoid of green.   (29)

For a while I stand
To watch antelopes
Roaming about freely
In the wasteland spread out
As far as my eyes can see.   (30)

Returning Home

After a journey of half a year
I am coming home,
And now I see
Through a rift in the clouds
The Land of the Rising Sun.   (31)

Moment by moment,
The quarters of a city in my
          homeland
Look larger.
From the cockpit
I gaze at them, fascinated.   (32)

1954

Woods

> Having returned from my journey,
> I sojourn in Karuizawa,
> Where the woods
> In autumn tints overflow
> With the atmosphere of my homeland.
>
> *(33)*

Recalling the United Kingdom

> Since I went
> To the United Kingdom
> For the coronation,
> How quickly
> This one year has passed!　　　　*(34)*

> How beautiful it must be
> At this time of the year!
> Occasionally,
> I remember
> London in early summer.　　　　*(35)*

33　Title: theme for the New Year's Poetry Reading.
　　Karuizawa: a fashionable summer retreat since the late 1800s, on a plateau
900 to 1,000 metres above sea level, in eastern Nagano Prefecture.

1955

A Fountain

Green is the moss
At the bottom of the fountain,
Its crystalline water
Welling forth
Into a silent stream.   *(36)*

The Autumn Sky

The sky of autumn
Spreads over the mountains,
Peak after peak,
Extending far beyond them,
Unmarred by any cloud.   *(37)*

---

36 Title: theme for the New Year's Poetry Reading.
37 Title: theme marking the coming-of-age of Prince Masahito, the younger
brother of Emperor Akihito. Following his marriage in 1963, the title of
Prince Hitachi was conferred on him by the Emperor.

1956

Early Spring

As the ice
Over the brook melts,
The first stream
Of frothing water
Now races over rocks.   (38)

1957

Fire

As the fires
Quietly burn at Shinkaden,
In a low tone
I hear the singing voices echo
To the strains of the koto.   (39)

38 Title: theme for the New Year's Poetry Reading.
39 Title: theme for the New Year's Poetry Reading.
   At Niinamesai, an annual rite, performed on November 23, in which the
Emperor makes an offering of newly harvested rice to Amaterasu Ōmikami,
the progenitor of the Imperial Family, and then himself partakes of the offering.
   Shinkaden: a shrine in the Imperial Palace where the Niinamesai rite is
performed.
   Koto: a Japanese musical instrument similar to a zither. The one used at
Niinamesai has six strings stretched over an oblong board.

Wisteria in Bloom

Fresh is the verdure
Of May
In the Palace garden,
Where, crowned with young leaves,
White wisteria clusters hang down. *(40)*

The Sakuma Dam

Having watched the film
On the construction of the dam,
I visit the site
And, with the dam before my eyes,
Think of those days.   *(41)*

The wall of the dam,
For which many lives
Have been sacrificed,
Rises high
In a valley between mountains.   *(42)*

---

40 Title: theme for the birthday of Emperor Showa.

41, 42 Sakuma Dam: a gravity dam that produces hydroelectricity, it is located
in the middle reaches of the Tenryū River, Shizuoka Prefecture. It is one
of Japan's largest dams, with an embankment 155.5 metres high. There
were ninety-four fatalities associated with its construction, which was com-
pleted in 1956.

1958

Clouds

> A cirrus cloud,
> Floating alone
> In the wide sky,
> Draws after it
> Numerous fine threads.   *(43)*

The Opening Ceremony

> With a burst of applause
> The flag of Afghanistan
> Comes into view.
> The Asian Games
> Have now commenced.   *(44)*

43 Title: theme for the New Year's Poetry Reading.
44–46 On the Asian Games

The Closing Ceremony

The sacred flame extinguished,
Torches appear in a row
In the grand stadium,
Where gently there flow
Strains of 'By Fireflies' Glow'.   (45)

Answering the applause
From the stands,
The departing athletes,
In their own ways,
Wave their hands.   (46)

In Hokkaidō

Out in the suburbs,
Leaves of trees are light green,
Making me feel
As if we were driving
Through mountains of Honshū.   (47)

---

45 'By Fireflies' Glow': a Japanese farewell song to the melody of *Auld Lang Syne*.
47 Honshū: the largest of Japan's four main islands, covering an area of about 227,400 square kilometres.

Having passed over
A mountain in hazy rain,
I come to a valley,
Where a mining town
Is crowded with houses.   (48)

Sandhills,
Thick with *sukashiyuri*
And *hamanasu*, roll on.
Calm and white is
The Sea of Okhotsk.   (49)

After the Decision on Betrothal

As I continue
My talks with her,
I become aware
That, in my heart,
A window is opening.   (50)

49 *Sukashiyuri: Lilium maculatum.*
    Hamanasu: Rosa rugosa.
50 Decision: According to the Imperial Law, the Imperial Household Council
    must give its approval prior to the marriage of members of the Imperial Family.

1959

Window

> Seen from the window,
> Leaves of *mokkoku,*
> Shining white in the light
> Of the wintry sun,
> Sway in the breeze.   *(51)*

The Visit to Ise Grand Shrine after the Wedding

> Looking up
> At high branches of cryptomeria,
> Thick and dark green,
> I walk along the way
> Approaching the shrine.   *(52)*

---

51 Title: theme for the New Year's Poetry Reading.
   Mokkoku: an evergreen tree, *Ternstroemia japonica.*
52 Ise Grand Shrine: located in Ise City, Mie Prefecture, it comprises an Inner
   Shrine and an Outer Shrine. The Inner Shrine is consecrated to Amaterasu
   Ōmikami. See Emperor's poem *39.*
   Cryptomeria: a large evergreen tree, the *Cryptomeria japonica,* or Japanese
   cedar, may reach a height of forty-five metres and is grown for its valuable
   soft wood.

Having walked in the shade of trees
Along the path leading
To the sacred precincts,
I behold the new shrine
Bright in the morning sun.   *(53)*

1960

Light

At midday
Sunlight penetrates
The depths of woods,
Dappling the carpet of fallen leaves
Beneath the oak trees.   *(54)*

53 New shrine: as tradition dictates, the Inner and Outer Shrines are razed and
   rebuilt every twenty years on adjacent sites.   The 'new shrine' was built in
   1953.
54 Title: theme for the New Year's Poetry Reading.

Spring Sky

> As budding catkins
> Begin to hang down,
> The white birch treetops
> Are inlaid with the sky
> Of early spring. (55)

1961

Youth

> Each time I see
> White birches,
> The growth of their fresh buds
> Captivates my eyes with
> The savour of maturing spring. (56)

---

55 Title: theme for the birthday of the Empress Dowager (1903–), mother
of Emperor Akihito.
56 Title: theme for the New Year's Poetry Reading.

In Iran

> At the end of the road,
> Which runs through
> Mountains and plains of red soil,
> The car approaches
> The pillars of Persepolis.   *(57)*

In Ethiopia

> In the grassland
> Extending before my eyes,
> Scattered here and there,
> Flat-topped
> Acacias grow.   *(58)*

> Seeing the acacia trees
> With nests of birds
> Hanging from their branches,
> I deeply feel
> I am in Africa.   *(59)*

> As the black dots
> Draw nearer, they assume
> Discernible shapes:
> They are flocks of oryx
> In the savannah.   *(60)*

Earth

Day by day, it is warmer:
Day by day, the snow melts away.
From beneath the snow
The moist earth of early spring
Appears at last, today.   *(61)*

Marine Blue

As I gaze at
The morning sea
From the side of the boat,
Bullet mackerel dart
Through the marine blue.   *(62)*

61 Title: theme for the New Year's Poetry Reading.
62 Title: theme for the birthday of Emperor Showa.

1963

Grassland

> Through stretches
> Of vast grassland
> In Africa,
> I proceed, stooping
> In pursuit of oryx. (*63*)

1964

Paper

> Examining
> Our collection
> Of Japanese paper,
> We voice our thoughts
> On how each was made. (*64*)

---

63 Title: theme for the New Year's Poetry Reading.
   Visiting Ethiopia.
64 Title: theme for the New Year's Poetry Reading.

Fields in Bloom

> On the plateau,
> Spikes of eulalia bending
> At the mercy of the wind,
> Show flowers in bloom
> Not seen in summer.   *(65)*

1965

Birds

> From a wood in winter
> A lone bird takes wing,
> Seen against a bank of clouds
> Stretching adrift
> In vermilion layers.   *(66)*

---

65 Title: theme for the wedding of Prince Masahito.   See Emperor's poem *37*.
    Eulalia: a tall, perennial grass. *Miscanthus sinensis.*
66 Title: theme for the New Year's Poetry Reading.
68 Miao: people inhabiting the mountainous areas of southwestern China and
    northern parts of Vietnam, Laos and Thailand.   They are known for their
    use of the slash-and-burn method of agriculture to grow corn and rice.

In Thailand

Looking down
On forest after forest
I see the single thread
Of the Mekong flowing
White and glittering.   *(67)*

Together with
The King and Queen of Thailand,
It is towards
A village of the tribe of Miao
That we are setting forth.   *(68)*

By the mountain pass
Leading to the village
Of the tribe of Miao,
My wife found
Tsurifune flowers.   *(69)*

Walking downhill,
Enjoying mountain flowers
In bloom along the pass,
We came to a hamlet
With all the trees burnt down.   *(70)*

---

69 *Tsurifune: Impatiens textori*, an annual plant of the *Balsaminaceae* family,
genus *Impatiens*.   Similar species grow in Thailand.

1966

Voice

> Among the voices
> Of children frolicking,
> I hear distinctly louder than the rest
> The voice of my own son,
> Calling to his mother.   *(71)*

A Dove

> In my childhood days,
> On the way to school
> I often heard the cooing
> Of the turtledove,
> As my son may also hear it now.   *(72)*

71 Title: theme for the New Year's Poetry Reading.
72 Title: theme for the birthday of the Empress Dowager.

Flag

> I hear
> The sound of flags flapping,
> Held by a crowd
> Thronging the vast lawn
> To celebrate this happy day.   *(73)*

Condolences on the Death of Dr. Shinzo Koizumi

> As I pause for a while,
> Sitting before
> The altar,
> There echoes in my ears
> His voice as I used to hear it.   *(74)*

---

73 Title: theme for the birthday of Emperor Showa.
   People came in crowds to the Palace grounds to greet Emperor Showa on
   his birthday.
74 Dr. Shinzo Koizumi (1888–1966): an economist, educator, author and the
   president of Keiō University from 1933 until 1947. He served as an adviser
   to Emperor Akihito from 1946 until his demise.

1967

Fish

    Having laid
    Eggs on the glass
    Of the aquarium,
    The parent tilapias
    Take turns in watching them.   *(75)*

In Peru

    The motorway winds up
    Along the Rimac River
    Which flows,
    Carving gorges,
    Through the Andes Mountains.   *(76)*

75 Title: theme for the New Year's Poetry Reading.
   Tilapia: genus of African freshwater fish of the *Cichlidae* family.

1968

A River

> Over yonder, where
> These waters flow,
> Lies the Amazon's estuary.
> I dip my hand into the stream
> And find it a bit cool to the touch.   *(77)*

1969

Star

> The Southern Cross,
> A name familiar to my ears
> In childhood—
> Now I have seen it
> In the night sky of Peru.   *(78)*

77 Title: theme for the New Year's Poetry Reading.
    Visiting Brazilia.
78 Title: theme for the New Year's Poetry Reading.

In the Garden

Waiting for spring,
Countless catkins
Are growing,
Hanging from high branches
Of the alder tree.   *(79)*

1970

Flowers

All over the castle ruins,
Yellow flowers
Are in full bloom.
Wondeirng what they may be,
I walk up among them.   *(80)*

80 Title: theme for the New Year's Poetry Reading.
81 Title: theme for the birthday of Emperor Showa.
81, 82 World Exposition: Japan World Exposition, Osaka 1970.

Blue Sky

In the morning sunshine
The snow by the roadside
Is glittering,
As under a clear blue sky
The world exposition opens.   *(81)*

Meiji Shrine's Golden Anniversary

The Emperor
Laid the foundation
Of the state
In which the world exposition
Is now in bloom.   *(82)*

Near Lake Chūzenji

Swimming upstream
In a brook which flows
Into the lake,
A trout takes a rest
Under a bridge.   *(83)*

---

82 Meiji Shrine: A Shinto shrine in Tokyo dedicated to the spirits of Emperor
    Meiji (1852–1912) and his consort, Empress Shoken (1850–1914).
83 Lake Chūzenji: in Tochigi Prefecture, 1,269 metres above sea level, it covers
    11.5 square kilometres.

In Iwate Prefecture

The smoke of burning straw
Drifts over the stretch of paddy,
As evening falls
In the countryside
Of Michinoku. *(84)*

With synchronized steps,
The disabled athletes
March in;
A storm of applause resounds
In the stadium of Michinoku. *(85)*

At Lake Tazawa

When still a child
I learned that Lake Tazawa
Was a habitat of *kunimasu.*
Along its shore where I now walk
What silence reigns! *(86)*

84, 85 On a National Sports Festival for the Disabled. Prefectures take turns in hosting the annual event.
  Michinoku: a district comprising the present Aomori, Iwate, Miyagi and Fukushima Prefectures.
86, 87 Lake Tazawa: Japan's deepest lake, located in Akita Prefecture.
86 Kunimasu: an extinct fish, of the genus *Oncorhynchus*, that was once endemic in the lake.

Coming and going,
Water gently laps
Upon the rocks on the shore.
Reddened with maple leaves
Is Lake Tazawa in the rain.   *(87)*

On Niinamesai

Walking
Along the verandah
Lit by torches,
I find myself
Thinking of ancient times.   *(88)*

The rites
Of Niiname having commenced,
In Shinkaden
A melody played on *hichiriki*
Flows gently.   *(89)*

88–94 On Niinamesai. See Emperor's poem 39.
89 Shinkaden: see Emperor's poem 39.
89, 90 *Hichiriki*: a short (18 cm.), double-reed Japanese wind instrument, used mainly in ancient music performed at the Imperial court and important shrines and temples.

In harmony
With the melody
Of *hichiriki*
A voice singing in low tones
Floats in the silence.   (90)

As the tone
Of the singing rises,
I find myself
Gazing at the small
Flame of a lamp.   (91)

As the singing voice
Passes into silence,
I now hear
The serene voice of the Emperor
Reading his prayer.   (92)

After worshipping,
I resume my seat,
And for a while, I wait,
Hearing the many footsteps
Of those in attendance.   (93)

The evening rites
Having come to an end,
I wend my way back,
Hearing the singing voices
Still faintly flowing.   (94)

1971

Home

> There resounds in the home
> For the physically handicapped
> The tune of 'Going Home',
> Played wholeheartedly
> On various instruments.　　　　*(95)*

1972

Mountains

> On a rolling stretch
> Of bare mountains, I see
> Many a trail—
> The tracks left by men
> And beasts that have passed through.　*(96)*

95 Title: theme for the New Year's Poetry Reading.
   Visiting a rehabilitation centre for the disabled in Iwate Prefecture.
   'Going Home': the opening melody of the second movement of Anton
   Dvorak's *Symphony No. 9*, or *New World Symphony*.
96 Title: theme for the New Year's Poetry Reading.
   Visiting Afghanistan.

1973

Child

Eyes round with wonder,
Staring at the plant,
My little child tells me that
On the stems of the windmill palm,
He has found thorns!   *(97)*

1974

Morning

As I proceed
Along the verandah to Shinden,
The first gleam
Of dawn appears in the sky
Of New Year's Day.   *(98)*

---

97 Title: theme for the New Year's Poetry Reading.
98 Title: theme for the New Year's Poetry Reading.
   At Saitansai, the New Year rites which require that, early on New Year's
Day, the Emperor and the Crown Prince worship at the three shrines at
the Imperial Palace, namely, Kashikodokoro, dedicated to Amaterasu Ōmi-
kami; Kōreiden dedicated to the preceding emperors, empresses and members
of the Imperial Family; and Shinden, dedicated to all heavenly, earthly and
other divinities.

Firmament

> With the smoke
> Of fireworks drifting
> In the firmament,
> The national sports festival
> Skiing events now commence.　　*(99)*

Seeing Prince Naruhito off to Australia

> How quickly time flies!
> Fifteen years
> Have glided past,
> And now my son is ascending
> The airplane ramp.　　*(100)*

99　Title: theme for the birthday of Emperor Showa.
　　On the skiing events at the Winter National Sports Festival in Fukushima
　　Prefecture.
100　Prince Naruhito: the Crown Prince of Japan and the eldest son of Emperor
　　Akihito.

1975

Festival

Amidst songs
Of praise to the gods
I hear the voice
Of worship by the Emperor
On the night of Niiname.　　　　*(101)*

Vermilion

As we gather
At an evening banquet
For visitors from a foreign land,
Layered clouds
Flow like vermilion flags.　　　　*(102)*

101 Title: theme for the New Year's Poetry Reading.
　　Niiname: Niinamesai, see Emperor's poem *39*.
102 Title: theme for the birthday of the Empress Dowager.
　　At a dinner at the Imperial Palace in the Hōmeiden Room, a wall of which
features a tapestry depicting layered clouds.

Voices

> To welcome me,
> A visitor from a foreign land,
> Children's voices
> Resound with the melody
> Of 'Moon over the Castle Ruins'. *(103)*

In Nepal

> With red blooms,
> Rhododendron trees appear
> Here and there
> Along the path, as the car
> Proceeds on Mount Burchoki. *(104)*

103 Title: theme for the birthday of Emperor Showa.
   Visiting Nepal.
   'Moon Over the Castle Ruins': a popular song, the music of which was composed by Rentaro Taki (1879–1903), based on a poem by Bansui Doi (1871–1952).
104 On the coronation of H.M. King Birendra.

In Okinawa Prefecture

War flames
Burnt up
The hill of Mabuni,
Which, thirty years later,
I am now ascending.   (105)

Over the path
To the well where the lives
Of many were lost
In the War, trees
Have grown so thickly.   (106)

Three decades
Have already passed since
The War ended.
I think over and over again
Of this hill.   (107)

105-107 On the opening of the International Ocean Exposition.
105 Hill of Mabuni: on the main island of Okinawa, it is the site of the last
World War II ground battle.

1976

A Slope

Along the slope of Mabuni
Thirty years have flowed.
In this time of peace
I feel that there is nothing
So precious as life.   *(108)*

In Jordan

As I set out with
The King of this foreign land
On the dusky sea,
From behind a rocky mountain
The full moon rises.   *(109)*

Standing on the shore
By the clear water,
I look toward the offing,
Where the sea off Aqaba
Swarms with large vessels.   *(110)*

---

108 Title: theme for the New Year's Poetry Reading.
    Mabuni: see Emperor's poem *105*.

1977

Ocean

Seen from the Cape
Of Ashizuri, far in the distance
Where the Japan Current flows,
The vast expanse of ocean
Shines bright.   (111)

In Aomori Prefecture

The boat is gliding
Smoothly along Mutsu Bay,
Leaving behind
The voices of people
Giving us a hearty send-off.   (112)

111 Title: theme for the New Year's Poetry Reading.
    Cape Ashizuri: southernmost point of Shikoku Island.
    Japan Current: also known as the Black Current or *kuroshio*, it is a
branch of the Pacific Ocean equatorial current that influences climate.
112 On the Summer National Sports Festival.
    Mutsu Bay: on the north coast of Aomori Prefecture, northern Honshū.

In Aomori Prefecture

At the gathering
Of disabled athletes, with them
I watch the figure formation
Of an *asunaro* tree
Spreading over the lawn.   *(113)*

1978

Mother

What peace overflows
The features of the child
When it is asleep
Under the tender care
Of its own loving mother.   *(114)*

113 On a National Sports Festival for the Disabled.
      Asunaro: *Thujopsis dolabrata*, a Japanese evergreen often up to 35 metres
   tall.   It is the official tree of Aomori Prefecture.
114 Title: theme for the New Year's Poetry Reading.

Swans

> Every year
> Still more lakes
> Are visited by swans—
> A testimony
> To a peaceful era.　　　　　*(115)*

In Brazil

> People descended
> From the Land of the Rising Sun
> Fill the scene of the ceremony
> Progressing in exaltation
> Under Brazilian skies.　　　*(116)*

> In this foreign land
> I meet people gathered who share
> My ancestors' blood,
> And with them I look back
> Over the passage of seventy years.　*(117)*

---

115 Title: theme for the birthday of Emperor Showa.

116–17 On the ceremony marking the seventieth anniversary of Japanese immigration to Brazil. In June 1908, 781 Japanese landed in Santos and, by the early 1980s, the number of Japanese nationals and their descendants living in Brazil had reached over eight hundred thousand representing the largest community of Japanese outside Japan.

1979

Hill

> The water foaming
> On the beach at the foot
> Of the hills of Sangaoka,
> Grass puffers draw nearer
> In the flow of the flood tide.   *(118)*

In Romania

> As an autumn evening
> Is about to fall
> In Suceava,
> On the fields of bare soil
> Not a figure can be seen.   *(119)*

---

118 Title: theme for the New Year's Poetry Reading.
   Sangaoka hills: in the town of Hayama, Kanagawa Prefecture.   There is
an Imperial Villa in the town.
   Grass puffer: a large shoal of these, or *Takifugu niphobles*, spawn on the
gravelly beach during the May–July flood tides.
119 Suceava: a county in northeastern Romania.

In Bulgaria

> Waves surging
> On the Black Sea
> In the deepening autumn,
> Jellyfish are adrift
> Amid shadows of an embankment.   *(120)*

1980

Cherry Blossoms

> Almost four years
> Have passed
> Since the time I saw
> The red cherry blossoms
> Amid the ruins of Nakijin.   *(121)*

121 Title: theme for the New Year's Poetry Reading.
     Nakijin ruins: the ruins of Nakijin Castle, on the main island of Okinawa.
     The castle was the seat of the kings of northern Okinawa.

Lily Magnolia

> It was planted
> Not many years ago,
> This small lily magnolia
> On whose upper twigs
> Flowers are beginning to bloom.   *(122)*

Meiji Shrine's Sixtieth Anniversary

> At the celebration
> Of the centennial, I recall
> The deeds done
> By the pioneers, while pondering on
> The reign of Emperor Meiji.   *(123)*

In Tochigi Prefecture

> Sitting in wheelchairs,
> Children play pianicas
> Whose melody resounds
> In the school grounds
> On an autumn day.   *(124)*

---

122 Title: theme for the birthday of Emperor Showa.
Lily magnolia: *Magnolia liliflora.*
123 On the centenary ceremony of the Japan Federation of Engineering Societies.
124 On a National Sports Festival for the Disabled.

Sounds

> To the sound
> Of creaking, groaning
> Wheelchairs,
> The basketball court
> Is filled with cheering.   *(125)*

New Year's Day

> With my son who has
> Come of age,
> I proceed to the Imperial Palace
> Under the clear sky
> Of New Year's Day.   *(126)*

125 Title: theme for the New Year's Poetry Reading.
126 My son: Prince Naruhito.   See Emperor's poem *100*.

Cherry Bream

Raised with a view to
Making the ocean abound
With cherry bream,
Young ones, in shoals,
Go swimming out to sea.   (127)

1982

A Bridge

From the train window
I see the inner Lake Hamana
Far in the distance,
Where the bridge of the Tōmei
    motorway
Clearly appears.   (128)

127 Title: theme for the birthday of Emperor Showa.
     Cherry bream: red sea bream in the spawning season, around cherry-
     blossom time.
128 Title: theme for the New Year's Poetry Reading.
     Lake Hamana: in southwestern Shizuoka Prefecture.
     Tōmei motorway: completed in 1969, it links Tokyo and Nagoya.

Spring Wind

> With my father and mother
> I have come out
> In the spring sea.
> With the wind blowing,
> We set out for Tateishi.   *(129)*

In Shimane Prefecture

> From the far distance
> Canoes come gliding
> Along the river,
> Their paddles so lightly
> Touching the water.   *(130)*

---

129 Title: theme for the birthday of the Empress Dowager.
   Tateishi: a beach, three kilometres southeast of the Imperial Villa in Hayama,
Kanagawa Prefecture.
130 On the Summer National Sports Festival.

64

In Shimane Prefecture

Having spent a night
By Lake Shinji, in the morning
I see a small boat come
And then turn round in the lake,
While fishing for freshwater clams.   *(131)*

The athletes,
Overcoming obstacles,
Have gathered.
Feeling their delight,
I watch their races and games.   *(132)*

Among the physically handicapped
Marching in the stadium,
There is one
Accompanied by his guide dog
Trotting beside him.   *(133)*

131–33 On a National Sports Festival for the Disabled.
131 Lake Shinji: in northeastern Shimane Prefecture, connected to the Sea of
Japan by the man-made Sada River.

In Hyōgo Prefecture

Sailing out to sea
With people gathered
From various places,
I release young sea bream
Into the waters of Kasumi.　　　*(134)*

On Iriomote Island

At the southern isle
Of Iriomote
Were caught goby
Which I named *Kuro-obi-haze*.
Then I described them.　　　*(135)*

As in succession
New kinds of goby are discovered,
I start wondering
About the future
Of this southern island.　　　*(136)*

---

134 On the National Festival for the Cherished Sea.
　　Kasumi: a scenic town on the Sea of Japan coast.
135, 136 Iriomote Island: located 450 kilometres southwest of the main island
of Okinawa, it is hilly with 400-metre-high mountains. Ninety-six per cent
covered in subtropical forests, the island has mangroves flourishing at its river
mouths and is rich in fauna which includes the Iriomote *yamaneko*, a wildcat
endemic to the island.

1983

Island

> Ready to be launched
> Shortly into the sky,
> The rocket stands
> At the extreme south
> Of the island.   *(137)*

In Gumma Prefecture

> On the basketball court
> Athletes in wheelchairs
> Rejoice
> Over victory,
> Holding each other's hands.   *(138)*

135 *Kuro-obi-haze*: *Myersina nigrivirgata*, a black-belt goby.
  Describing them: Emperor Akihito described the goby in a paper entitled *Myersina nigrivirgata, a New Species of Goby from Okinawa Prefecture, Japan*, published in the *Japanese Journal of Ichthyology*, March 10, 1983.
137 Title: theme for the New Year's Poetry Reading.
  Island: Tanegashima, the site of the Tanegashima Space Center, in Kagoshima Prefecture.
138 On a National Sports Festival for the Disabled.

1984

Green

A variety of lives
Have been protected and
Fostered here,
On Iriomote Island
Which stands clad in green.   *(139)*

The Silver Jubilee

Our wedding
Was held as long as
A quarter of a century ago.
And yet, so clear in my mind's eye
Are the scenes of that day in
   full bloom.   *(140)*

139 Title: theme for the New Year's Poetry Reading.
     Iriomote Island: see Emperor's poem *135*.
140 Wedding: April 10, 1959.

In Belgium

> Also with us
> Was the Queen of the Netherlands;
> The night
> At the palace in Belgium
> Passed so quickly.   *(141)*

In Senegal

> Having flown
> Over blue oceans
> And a vast dry land,
> The plane approaches
> The airport of Dakar.   *(142)*

> At Goree Island,
> Where countless slaves
> Had been shipped,
> I ponder over the passage
> Of the history of man.   *(143)*

---

141 En route to Senegal and Zaire.
143 Goree Island: south of Cape Vert, Senegal, it is one of the earliest European
settlements in western Africa. For three hundred years, some twenty
million Africans were shipped through the island to the Americas.

I gaze over the vast dry land,
Together with someone
Who came to raise vegetables
In Senegal, a country
Far from her homeland. *(144)*

Water drawn up
From a well with a bucket
Sinks into
The dry soil
Of a farm in Senegal. *(145)*

In Zaire

Constructed
With the toil and sweat of men
From the Land of the Rising Sun,
The bridge of Matadi
Spans a muddy stream. *(146)*

---

146 Matadi: a port city on the Congo River and 150 kilometres inland from
the Atlantic coast port of Banana in western Zaire.

An Earthquake in Western Nagano Prefecture

The mountainside
Gouged away by a landslide
In the wake of an earthquake. . . .
And the graphic scar
Is shown on television.   *(147)*

1985

Journey

On the morning of my journey,
Looking from my window,
There I saw Mount Iwate
Rising before my eyes,
Its foot coloured by maple leaves.   *(148)*

148 Title: theme for the New Year's Poetry Reading.
      Mount Iwate: a 2,041-metre peak in Iwate Prefecture.

71

In Spain

Four centuries ago
Boys from Japan
Visited El Escorial,
Which I am now gazing on
From the sky.   *(149)*

As we circle in the sky
Over El Escorial
The people
Are waving flags
To welcome our helicopter.   *(150)*

In Sweden

At Uppsala, as I look through
The letters, I muse over
The development of relations
Between this foreigner
And people of Japan.   *(151)*

---

149 Boys from Japan: In February 1582, a mission comprising four Japanese
boys was sent to visit the court of Philip II of Spain and Pope Gregory
XIII. They visited El Escorial in 1584 and returned to Japan in 1590.
151 On seeing letters sent by Katsuragawa Hoshu and Nakagawa Ju-an at
Uppsala University.

In Norway

Among the villagers
Gathered on the shores
Of a fjord,
A compatriot of ours
Had also come to see us.   *(152)*

With the King of Norway
I rambled in a park,
Where the air
Was suffused with the mild
Sunshine of summer.   *(153)*

The Closing of the Kobe Universiad

To thunderous
Applause bursting across
The stadium,
Athletes enter,
The competitions now ended.   *(154)*

Katsuragawa Hoshu and Nakagawa Ju-an: Japanese physicians in the eighteenth century. Swedish physician and botanist Carl Peter Thunberg (1743–1828) visited Japan in 1775. During his one-year stay in Japan, he taught scholars, including Katsuragawa and Nakagawa, Western medicine, botany, zoology and astronomy. On his return to Sweden, he taught at Uppsala University.

In Hokkaidō

Innumerable stems
Of glasswort turning red
Stand in Lake Notoro
On whose shore a cold wind
Blows as evening falls.   *(155)*

The Return of Prince Naruhito from
Oxford University

Having spent
Two years at a university
In a foreign country,
My son has now
Come home again.   *(156)*

155 On the National Festival for the Cherished Sea.
    Glasswort: common name for plants of the genus *Salicornia* of the goose-
foot family. Native to salt marshes worldwide, the jointed, bright green
stems turn red in autumn.
    Lake Notoro: in northeastern Hokkaidō. Its northeastern reaches face the
Sea of Okhotsk.
156 Prince Naruhito: see Emperor's poem *100*.

In Ōita Prefecture

Amidst a storm
Of applause in the stadium,
There enter,
In a vigorous and close race,
Marathoners in wheelchairs.   *(157)*

At Cape Futtsu

In sand,
Blown by the wind,
The pine saplings
Planted thirty years ago
Have grown into a grove.   *(158)*

---

157 On the International Wheelchair Marathon in Ōita Prefecture, north-eastern Kyūshū.
158 On the Silviculture Festival.
Cape Futtsu: extends for three kilometres at the gate of Tokyo Bay in southwestern Chiba Prefecture.

After the Coming-of-Age Ceremony

Having come of age,
My son left
For Ise
In the morning,
Soon after the dawn.   *(159)*

1986

Water

Returning from a journey
In foreign lands,
I feel what a blessing
Is the abundance
Of water in Japan.   *(160)*

---

159 My son: Prince Fumihito, the second son of Emperor Akihito. Following
   his marriage in 1990, the title of Prince Akishino was conferred on him by the
   Emperor.
      Ise: see Emperor's poem 52.
160 Title: theme for the New Year's Poetry Reading.

Ryūka (1975-76)

Kompaku no Tō

Let me offer these flowers
To you, unknown souls,
Praying from my heart
For a world without war.   *(161)*

Mabuni

I visit the old battlefields,
Where grass and trees have grown dense,
Again and again
My thoughts going back to the War. *(162)*

161-66 Ryūka: see p. 8.
161 Kompaku no Tō: literally meaning a 'monument of souls', it is dedicated
to the 35,000 unknown soldiers and civilians killed in Okinawa during
World War II.   At the time, the ashes of war dead had been laid to rest there.
The monument is on Itoman Beach, on the main island of Okinawa, where
the fiercest battle on Okinawa was fought.
162 Mabuni: see Emperor's poem *105.*

At Airaku-en

Singing a song
For a departing traveller,
They saw us off, on their faces
The unforgettable smiles.   *(163)*

Now they begin to sing
The song for a departing traveller.
How deeply impressed on my mind
Is this island thick with *yūna*!   *(164)*

On Ie Island

Farmlands spread out below,
Mount Gusuku soaring above,
Overwhelming sorrow wells up
   in my mind
With thoughts of the War.   *(165)*

163 Airaku-en: a hospital in Nago City, on the main island of Okinawa, spe-
   cializing in the treatment of Hansen's disease.
164 *Yūna*: the yellowish flowers of the *Hibiscus filiaceus*, found in Okinawa.
165 Ie Island: just off the coast of the main island of Okinawa and site of fierce
   fighting during World War II, it is mostly flat except for Mount Gusuku.

Nakijin Castle Ruins

Stepping inside the gate
Of Nakijin Castle,
I see cherry blossoms
Blooming in rosy hue.   *(166)*

166 Nakijin Castle: see Emperor's poem *121*.

EMPRESS MICHIKO

1960

Spring Sky

> As I look up
> At the plum blossoms
> Becoming tinged with colour,
> My face turns upward
> To the gentle sky of spring. $\qquad$ (1)

Young Grass

> As you leave the royal garden,
> Princess, how refreshingly
> The grass buds forth
> Along your new path—
> In the youthfulness of spring. $\qquad$ (2)

---

1 Title: theme for the birthday of the Empress Dowager.
   Empress Dowager: see Emperor's poem 55.
   Plum: the tree, a species of apricot, is commonly translated as plum in
English.
2 Title: theme for the wedding of Princess Takako, the younger sister of
   Emperor Akihito.

On the Birth of Prince Naruhito

Like a treasure
Entrusted to me,
Even though he is my baby,
There are times when I am aware
Of holding him in my arms with awe. *(3)*

1961

Verdure

Coming from far away,
Crossing the seas,
The ōtani watari
Has at last sprouted forth
New verdure! *(4)*

3 Prince Naruhito: see Emperor's poem *100*.
4 Title: theme for the sixtieth birthday of Emperor Showa.
   Emperor Showa: see Emperor's poem *13*.
   Ōtani watari: bird's-nest fern.

On the demise of Mrs. Shigeko Higashikuni

At this moment
When a new life sublime
Commences for her,
I lay by her feet the shoes
For another journey.   *(5)*

1962

Earth

Awakened at midnight,
Suddenly I feel a fondness
For the smell of the earth in spring,
While I listen to frosty leaves
Scattering all night long.   *(6)*

5 Mrs. Shigeko Higashikuni: the eldest sister of Emperor Akihito.
    The waka alludes to the custom according to which objects that were both
    dear to the deceased in life and which are thought important for the journey
    to the hereafter are placed in the coffin.
6 Title: theme for the New Year's Poetry Reading.

85

Marine Blue

> Whence does it come—
> This tide of light
> Rushing in the springtime,
> And faintly filling
> The blue sky to overflowing!   *(7)*

At the Jiai-en Children's Home

> Far from my little ones,
> Leaving them behind
> As I travel on Mother's Day,
> It is the motherless children
> Who offer me their gift of songs.   *(8)*

---

7 Title: theme for the birthday of Emperor Showa.
8 In Kumamoto Prefecture.

1963

Grassland

As young farmers
Set their tractors plowing
The grassy plains,
Clods of earth intermingle
With lupinus flowers.   *(9)*

The Pearl

The pearl emits
A variety of colours
Within it,
Yet lucidly does it maintain
The colour of the ocean.   *(10)*

9 Title: theme for the New Year's Poetry Reading.
   Visiting an agricultural centre, Miyazaki Prefecture.
   Lupinus: lupine.   It is planted and ploughed into the earth as fertilizer.
10 Title: theme for the birthday of the Empress Dowager.

1964

Paper

The sunshine faintly
Falling on the braille paper
As the dots are typed,
Each letter rises,
Casting shadows on the page.   *(11)*

1965

Birds

One senses how soon
The grass blades will be sprouting
All over this hill,
For pheasants are now resting
On the soft, thawing earth.   *(12)*

---

11 Title: theme for the New Year's Poetry Reading.
12 Title: theme for the New Year's Poetry Reading.

Spring Tide

Already there is a softening
On the horizon,
And soon the Black Current
Will come pouring in,
Making the sea brim over.   (13)

On the Birth of Prince Fumihito

Three days have passed
Since his birth;
And around this new-born baby,
I now feel something of life
So vivid and fresh.   (14)

13 Title: theme for the birthday of Emperor Showa.
    Black Current: see Emperor's poem 111.
14 Prince Fumihito: see Emperor's poem 159.

1966

Voice

> It dawns upon me
> That he now speaks
> With the voice of a more grown-up boy.
> And he comes home trailing
> A faint smell of earth. (15)

Flag

> During these days
> While His Majesty is on a journey,
> Time and again I envisage
> His smile
> Amid the waving of flags. (16)

15 Title: theme for the New Year's Poetry Reading.
16 Title: theme for the birthday of Emperor Showa.

1967

Fish

On the blank space on the paper
Before me, my brush moves,
Forming the character 'sea',
On the day you, my prince, net in hand,
Search for fish along some shore.   *(17)*

On the Demise of a Teacher

Now left bereft,
With you no longer among us—
I recall those days when
Your presence brought a thaw,
Warming our hearts.   *(18)*

17 Title: theme for the New Year's Poetry Reading.
18 On a highly respected teacher, who taught Empress Michiko at university.

On the First Anniversary of the Death of
Dr. Shinzo Koizumi

> While the days seem
> To roll on as always,
> All of a sudden there comes to me
> The awareness, on this day in May,
> That you are no longer with us.   *(19)*

1968

A River

> The *terra roxa*
> Extends far beyond the horizon
> To where the Amazon flows.
> And my heart in sadness yearns
> For our dear countrymen dwelling
>   there.   *(20)*

19 Dr. Shinzo Koizumi: see Emperor's poem *74*.
20 Title: theme for the New Year's Poetry Reading.
    On a visit to Brazil the previous year.
    Terra roxa: the basaltic and diabasic rocks, so named for their reddish colour,
    which are found in some areas of Brazil.
    The poem reflects on the hardship suffered by those Japanese who have
    settled along the Amazon. See Emperor's poem *116*.

A Flower-drift

> Stretching both arms out
> To the sky, trying to catch
> The cherry blossom petals
> Snowdrifting in the wind;
> My child, too, dances in the spring. *(21)*

In Amami

> To while away the long path
> To school, children walk
> Chewing *amashiba* leaves.
> Oh, the sweet-sour flavour
> Of the tender, young leaves! *(22)*

---

21 Title: theme for the birthday of Emperor Showa.
22 Amami: officially called Amami Ōshima, in Kagoshima Prefecture, northeast of Okinawa.
   Amashiba: a large bush, found in the region of Okinawa, that has sweet-tasting leaves which children like to chew.

1969

Star

> The time-honoured ray
> That left a star
> Many a light-year ago
> Has this moment reached our Earth
> Preparing for its spring attire.   *(23)*

On the New Palace

> Happiness wells up
> In my heart
> As I look up at the Emperor
> Standing to greet the people
> From the high, newly built balcony. *(24)*

23 Title: theme for the New Year's Poetry Reading.
24 On the first time the people came to greet Emperor Showa on his birthday after the completion of the new Imperial Palace.

On the Birth of Princess Sayako

> Within the room
> Where the twilight creeps
> So softly in,
> Like a fragile petal lying,
> Lo! my little daughter sleeps.　　*(25)*

At the Sand Dunes Laboratory

> 'A sand dune moves
> As if it were alive!'
> A young scholar explains,
> His eyes glistening
> As he gazes into the distance.　　*(26)*

Withered Grass

> On the vast meadow
> Ruffled with withered grass
> In late autumn, I've come
> With my little one—amusing ourselves
> Stepping on each other's shadow.　　*(27)*

---

25 Princess Sayako: the daughter of Emperor Akihito.
26 In Tottori Prefecture.

1970

Flowers

> On the path
> Carpeted with young grass,
> For a moment I stand wondering—
> Then your voice reaches me
> From where forsythias are in bloom. *(28)*

Meiji Shrine's Golden Anniversary

> The light-blue sky
> That I am now gazing at!
> Is this not the scenery of the heart
> Which His Majesty
> Wished for us in his poem? *(29)*

---

28 Title: theme for the New Year's Poetry Reading.
29 Meiji Shrine: see Emperor's poem *82*.
    The poem alludes to one written by Emperor Meiji: If only the heart /
Could be as broad / As the wide-spreading / Transparently / Light-blue
sky!

Headland

> The wild horses
> Roaming on the headland of Toi
> So far away:
> Do not their very manes
> Bear the odour of the sea? (30)

Bush Clover

> Having tired of playing,
> My child returns home,
> Tiny flowers of the *hagi*
> Clinging here and there
> On her short, bobbed hair. (31)

The Flowers of the Tea Plant

> The white tea flower
> Blooms modestly,
> Always in deep shadow,
> Just reflecting the light
> Of its shiny leaves. (32)

---

30 Toi: a headland, in Miyazaki Prefecture, known for wild horses.
31 *Hagi*: bush clover.
32 Translated by Empress Michiko.

1971

Home

    Finally we are back
    In our motherland
    Where powdery snow is falling,
    And where our three loved ones
    Are waiting for us at home.   *(33)*

Recalling a Meeting with Some Young People

    With youthful eyes
    Shining clear, you talked
    About corneal transplants—
    A task to which you have
    Decided to dedicate your life.   *(34)*

33 Title: theme for the New Year's Poetry Reading.

A Monument

> Drenched in the rain,
> Together with bereaved families
> We pray for you who died at sea.
> Alas! more and more drenched,
> Must each of you be gone?   *(35)*

In Afghanistan

> In the faintly red glow
> Of the moon in Bamiyan,
> There stood
> The stone Buddhist image,
> Its face mutilated.   *(36)*

Winter Mountain

> One cold night, of a sudden,
> My son talks to me of the image
> That flashes in his mind's eye:
> Quiet trees covered with ice
> Standing on the winter mountain. *(37)*

---

35 A monument: erected at Kannonzaki, Kanagawa Prefecture, in memory of
those who perished at sea during World War II.   The inauguration took place
during a downpour.

36 Invaders professing another religion had mutilated the statue of Buddha.

1972

Mountains

> Along mountain paths
> Abounding with alpine blooms,
> People trudge,
> Greeting one another
> In friendly voices. (38)

The Ancient Burial Mound of Takamatsu

> O Prince, lying here in this tomb,
> Who could you be? What has
>   your slumber
> Been like all these years
> In the cool dimness of the stone vault
> Lit up with star signs painted on
>   the walls? (39)

38 Title: theme for the New Year's Poetry Reading.
39 Tomb: in Nara Prefecture, it was excavated in 1972 and dates back to
between the end of the seventh and the beginning of the eighth century.
  Star signs: the phrase refers to the ancient Chinese system of dividing the
stars into twenty-eight abodes, corresponding to the constellations. The
stone walls of the tomb are decorated with paintings representing these
abodes.

Above the muffled roar of the *Kuroshio*,
The sound of the foghorn
Announces
The birth of a new era
For the islands. *(40)*

A violent downpour of rain
Washes the hill of Mabuni
And nearby,
Where too, too many
Shed their blood. *(41)*

The island,
On which coral blossoms open
In succession,
Returns this midnight
Carrying all, even the children's
    slumber. *(42)*

40–42 The Okinawan islands continued to be under the administration of the United States of America even after the conclusion of the San Francisco Peace Treaty in 1951. They reverted to Japanese rule as the clock struck midnight, ushering in a new day on May 15, 1972. All vessels in Okinawa celebrated the event by sounding their foghorns.

40 *Kuroshio*: see Emperor's poem *111*.

41 Mabuni: see Emperor's poem *105*.

1973

Child

> In the garden
> Where the fragrance
> Of summer grass floats,
> So gently there falls a star
> Into the eye of my child. *(43)*

Field Fires

> Red flames
> Dart and sway
> Here and there—
> The burning of fields
> As in ancient days. *(44)*

43 Title: theme for the New Year's Poetry Reading.
44 Refers to the ancient custom of setting fields ablaze to prepare the ground for the next year's harvest.

Higan-zakura

The *higan-zakura*
Has given bloom
To a moment of early spring
On slender boughs
Of graceful mien.   *(45)*

Music

Soft strains
Of music
Tremble and flow from afar,
Court singers and dancers
Must be diligently rehearsing.   *(46)*

45 *Higan-zakura*: an early-flowering cherry. *Higan* is the equinoctial week,
   here referring to the spring equinox.
46 Title: theme for the birthday of the Empress Dowager.

Silkworms

> These spring silkworms,
> No doubt, have gone through
> Many rounds of sleep—
> Translucent white,
> They have begun to spin their thread.
>
> *(47)*

One Day

> As I gazed up at the magnolia
> Wondering which bough to choose,
> A flowering branch
> Lowered itself to me,
> Held in you hand, my lord.   *(48)*

47 The lifecycle of the silkworm involves five alternate phases of sleep and
   feeding before the worm reaches maturity when, its body translucent, it
   spins its cocoon.

The Passage of Autumn

Here, in this other hemisphere,
The month of June marks
The passage of autumn,
And brings early frost
To the garden.   (49)

In Chiba Prefecture

A handicapped athlete
Bears the torch high
As he runs
With the flame
Against the morning wind.   (50)

49 Title: theme for Culture Day (November 3).
    On recalling a visit to the Australian capital, Canberra, when Empress
    Michiko saw frost in June.
50 On the opening of a National Sports Festival for the Disabled.

Bonfire

He has passed away
Who, in a poem for children,
Immortalized the bonfire—
A bonfire of fallen leaves,
In a lane where camellias bloom.   *(51)*

The Milky Way in Winter

In the wintry sky
The Milky Way lets flow
    its stream of milk.
Oh, to think of you as still a babe
Soundly asleep
Under a sky like this.   *(52)*

51 Written in memory of the poet Seika Tatsumi, whose poem *Bonfire* has
   been set to music and is a well-known song.
52 On the birthday of Emperor Akihito.
   Translated by Empress Michiko.

1974

Morning

The transfer rites
Have been held in darkness.
And now I think of the dawn
Breaking peacefully into morning
On the Ise Shrines. *(53)*

Ears of Wheat

I think
Of ears of wheat swaying
In the fields of Koganei,
And I see you standing there
In your boyhood, my lord. *(54)*

53 Title: theme for the New Year's Poetry Reading.
   Ise Shrines: see Emperor's poem 52.
54 Koganei: the rural Tokyo district where Emperor Akihito lived from May
   1946 until December 1949.

A Birch Grove in Summer

> One after the other
> The children leave for school
> Trampling on dappled shadows
> Cast by the birch groves
> In early summer. (55)

Deer

> At the Gokoku Shrine
> An aged mother told me
> The dedicated one was her only son,
> Dear, as a deer's young,
> To its mother. (56)

---

55 Translated by Empress Michiko.

56 Gokoku Shrine: a name given to shrines, found nationwide, commemorating those who have dedicated their lives in some way to serving the country.

Deer's young: the phrase is used as a poetic device, or *makura kotoba* (literally a 'pillow word'), to convey the concept of an only son. The device is generally employed partly for amplification, to impart stylized imagery—much like the metaphor in Western rhetoric—and partly for sound, depending on the context. The stylized, semi-imagistic epithet, normally of five syllables, is used to modify certain fixed words.

Translated by Empress Michiko.

1975

Festival

> On the hills of Miwa
> And at the side of the River Sai,
> They must be holding rites
> In the shrines today
> To calm the spirits of flowers.   *(57)*

Festival

> Little ones repeatedly
> Touch the *Ojizō-sama*
> And then scatter flowers:
> A field festival
> Of childlike innocence.   *(58)*

57 Title: theme for the New Year's Poetry Reading.
   Miwa and River Sai: in Nara Prefecture.
   Rites: famous as a flower festival, they are held annually on April 18 at
Miwa Shrine and its affiliated neighbourhood shrines.   The line 'To calm the
spirits of flowers' suggests the desire to control diseases.
58 *Ojizō-sama*: this Bodhisattva, or enlightened one, is believed to watch over
children.

A Port

> I wonder
> From which direction
> Does this come—
> The sound of a faint foghorn
> Reaches our breakfast table.   (59)

Magnolias

> Upon uplifted petals
> Of half-blown magnolia blossoms
> Floating in the sky,
> The moon continues
> To shed her gentle beam.   (60)

Sea Breeze

> I think of those days of convalescence
> When I,
> Standing in the sea breeze,
> Saw the huge waves
> Break.   (61)

59 Translated by Empress Michiko.

The Colt

There was a song
About a colt
Reared for battle—
I was young,
The nation was at war.   *(62)*

The Pen

Among the fallen autumn leaves
Strewn on the ground
The child
Found a pheasant's feather
And made a pen of it.   *(63)*

63 Title: theme for Culture Day.

1976

A Slope

Despite their suffering,
People of this island
Are still so tender at heart;
Lost in this thought, I ascend
Their hill of *yūna* flowers.   *(64)*

Yellowtail

This must be the time
When the fishermen
Set out to sea
With the snow-thunder echoing
Under the Hokuriku sky.   *(65)*

64 Title: theme for the New Year's Poetry Reading.
   Yūna: see Emperor's poem *164*.
65 Hokuriku: an area comprising Fukui, Ishikawa, Toyama and Niigata pre-
   fectures skirting the Japan Sea coast where, in the period between the early
   winter rains and the first snowfalls, eerie, roaring claps of thunder can be
   heard at night. Residents of the area optimistically call the phenomenon
   buri-okoshi, or a yellowtail rouser, in the hope that yellowtail fishing will
   be good.
   Translated by Empress Michiko.

Childhood Days

> How young my mother was
> In this picture
> As she held me,
> Still so small, in her arms—
> Could it have been spring?   *(66)*

Tidings

> A message on tape
> In a clear, ringing voice
> Brings tidings
> From a blind woman,
> A koto player.   *(67)*

The Tower

> Overhead,
> Like a mass of crystallized prayer,
> A single wisp
> Of white cloud
> Floats above the tower.   *(68)*

67 Koto: see Emperor's poem *39.*
68 Title: theme for the birthday of Emperor Showa.

In Yugoslavia

Yellow blossoms are in full bloom
On this Adriatic coast
Where I have come today,
Accompanying the Prince,
His Majesty's emissary.   (69)

Winter Haze

Those white flowers
In the tea fields of Saga
Must be quietly blooming
In the misty haze
Of winter.   (70)

70 Saga: a prefecture, in northwestern Kyūshū, famous for tea.

1977

The Sea

When the lighthouses
On every cape softly glow
To illumine the sea,
How this country, seen from above,
Must glimmer: a lustrous bow!   *(71)*

New Moon

Closing the window
I stood for a while
In the evening air,
Steeped in the soft, tender rays
Of the new moon.   *(72)*

71 Title: theme for the New Year's Poetry Reading.
   Bow: alludes to the shape of the Japanese archipelago which, from the air,
   resembles the traditional bow used in martial arts.
72 Title: theme for the birthday of the Empress Dowager.
   Translated by Empress Michiko.

Floral Chill

> To my daughter
> As she set off
> To visit the blooming Ōshima cherry
> At the far end of the garden,
> I handed a warm wrap. (73)

Arrow-wheel

> Somebody has taken away
> The carp streamer from the pole
> And the lonely arrow-wheel
> Must now play all alone
> In the dusk. (74)

73 Floral chill: the sudden return of cold weather at blossom time in early spring.
74 Arrow-wheel: two circular devices which sit parallel, as a unit, atop a pole
to which streamers are attached. The unit, which turns in the wind, com-
prises a hub and vanes, each resembling the shaft of an arrow with its feathered
end pointing out toward the circumference. The unit, together with the
pole, a pennant and streamers, each depicting a carp, is called *koi-nobori* in
Japanese and is featured on May 5, Children's Day.
     Translated by Empress Michiko.

Arrowroot Blossoms

The arrowroot is blooming
In the shade of leaves.
May Her Majesty,
Laid low in scorching midsummer heat,
Find healing.   *(75)*

Sweet Acorns

As though in response
To my little one's joy,
Sweet acorns fall,
Hitting the steps
Again and again.   *(76)*

75 Written for the Empress Dowager who, at the time, was indisposed.

1978

Mother

Sorrows unrevealed
Even to us her children,
Mother must have had.
And yet, with what grace has she
Grown into her older years.   *(77)*

Bracken Sprouts

As he waited in the *lageri*
For the permit to return home,
Another spring would pass
With bracken sprouts
Turning into ferns.   *(78)*

77 Title: theme for the New Year's Poetry Reading.
78 On reading a collection of poems by one who was interned in Siberia for
   a long period of time in a *lageri*, a Russian word for a POW camp.

Chicks

Chicks,
Hatched in an incubator,
Cuddle for warmth
By the electric bulb in the box,
And sleep.   (*79*)

An Elegy for Miyoko Goto

From the heavenly skies
Look down now and see—
The cherry trees you so loved
Are blooming in succession
On the Japanese isles.   (*80*)

Swans

The swans and wild geese
Again take off on their journey,
Leaving behind
This island
Of spring.   (*81*)

---

80 Miyoko Goto: one of Empress Michiko's waka teachers, who said she
would like to travel through Japan, from south to north, following the
cherry blossom trail.

81 Title: theme for the birthday of Emperor Showa.

Minnows

The surface of the pond
Reflects the rich verdure.
A slight stir
As the minnows
Dart by.   (82)

Yachts

The awaited wind
Must have begun to blow.
Yachts, sailed by the young,
Now race by
Passing swiftly away.   (83)

The Lake

We made an early morning visit
To the eel farm by the lake,
Passing
By marshy land,
Where the reed warbler trills.   (84)

Snow Break

> The old people's home
> We visited that day
> In Akita—
> How are they faring now,
> In their shelter fenced in against the
>   snow?   *(85)*

1979

Hill

> To the Imperial Tombs
> On the hill,
> Before I journey across the sea,
> I go to offer sacred *sakaki*,
> Bedecked so rarely with flowers.   *(86)*

85 Akita: a prefecture in the north of the main island of Honshū.
   Snow break: A protective barrier of boards placed vertically around the
entrance of buildings or around entire buildings.
86 Title: theme for the New Year's Poetry Reading.
   Sakaki: a tree belonging to the tea family with small, drooping, yellowish-
white flowers that bloom in May and June. It is considered sacred in
Shintoism and sprigs of it are used as religious offerings.

Turn of the Year

> The year dawns—
> The sky, still aglow
> With last year's stars,
> As you, my lord, go forth
> To attend the Saitansai.　　　　　*(87)*

Seeds

> I gaze upon the white seeds
> I hold in the palm of my hand,
> Thinking that this year again
> They will grow and bloom,
> Scarlet safflowers wet with dew.　　*(88)*

The Morning Star

> Oh, this tranquillity
> Of the garden at dawn!
> The morning star above
> Sheds a soft, clear light
> In the cloudless sky.　　　　　*(89)*

---

87 Saitansai: see Emperor's poem *98*.
89 Title: theme for the birthday of Emperor Showa.

Water Lilies

> Fondly, I look back
> On the day you taught me
> The name of those flowers
> Blooming in the marshes of Nasu:
> *Hitsuji-gusa*, the lamb-flower.　　*(90)*

The Red Feathers

> I recall the strong glare of sunlight
> On that day in front of
> 　the railway station,
> A young student,
> I stood giving out
> Red feathers to passersby.　　*(91)*

---

90 *Hitsuji-gusa*: literally sheep-grass, it is a small, white flower of the water lily family, said to have been so named because it blooms at around two o'clock, the hour of the eighth sign (sheep) of the Oriental zodiac. The flower is used on Princess Sayako's crest. Princess Sayako: see Empress's poem *25*.

91 Red feathers: to be pinned on as badges, they are handed out by people collecting donations for charity from passersby on October 1 each year.

Excavation

I recognize my son
Among those who dig
At the site of a village,
Once buried under hot lava
In the Temmei era.   (92)

Evening Chill

Your garments,
As you return, my lord,
Having attended
The Shinjō rite,
Bear the cold chill of midnight.   (93)

Pots

Is this year, too,
Drawing to a close?
Salvation Army pots
Appear again
On the streets.   (94)

92 Title: theme for Culture Day.
    In 1783, Mount Asama, northwest of Tokyo, erupted and buried many
    villages.
    Temmei era: 1781–89.
93 Shinjō rite: Shinjōsai, also known as Niinamesai. See Emperor's poem 39.

1980

Cherry Blossoms

When the wind blows,
Snowdrifting cherry blossom petals
For a while
Come brightly shining
Between my daughter and me.　　　*(95)*

After the Rite of Kakan

Chōka

For this child who was granted life,
Born into this world that February evening,

Twenty years having passed,
Here and now he receives the crown.

He appears in a pale yellow garment;
His headgear, the *kūchōkokusaku* of
　　childhood, untied,

95　Title: theme for the New Year's Poetry Reading.
96　Kakan: the rite, celebrated on the Crown Prince's twentieth birthday,
　　marked his coming-of-age with the bestowal of headgear symbolizing adult-
　　hood.　One of the highlights of the ceremony was the snipping off of the
　　ends of the ties after they had been fastened.
　　　Chōka and hanka: see p. 8.

Firmly on his head is placed the new
   black crown.
The white ties, drawn down along
   his young cheeks,

Are fastened with care beneath his chin,
The loose ends snipped off with a loud clip.

These twenty years now belong to the past,
His childhood, to days gone by.

With a pure and clear heart, may he walk
From this day forth, along the straight,
   royal path

His ancestors walked, where he now stands
A full-grown Prince, O my son!

Hanka

A loud clip resounds
As the ties of his crown are snipped off—
My son stands.
How far in the past
That other February now seems.   *(96)*

Kūchōkokusaku: this headgear, representing childhood, is donned only by a
prince and only for the coming-of-age rite.

Spring Thaw

> I walk
> On the thawing, muddy road
> To see fresh spring shoots
> Emerging here and there
> On the embankment.   *(97)*

The Imperial Guard

> A young guard
> Stands at attention
> On a bright pavement
> Strewn with petals
> Along the banks of the moat.   *(98)*

Digging for Clams at Low Tide

> As the years pass,
> Memories of the sandy beach
> At low tide
> Where we played, digging for clams,
> Linger and grow.   *(99)*

Eighty-eighth Night

Wheat fields
Are already in the ears.
This year, again,
The time of 'the last frost'
Has come.   *(100)*

Mulberries

You placed
A ripe black mulberry
In the palm of my hand
And spoke, recalling the days
Of wartime evacuation.   *(101)*

100 Eighty-eighth night: refers to a day around May 1, eighty-eight days after
the beginning of spring which, according to the lunar calendar, is on about
February 4.
   'Last frost': an expression often used in literature referring to this time
of year, although the last frost actually comes much earlier.
101 During World War II, people were evacuated from the major cities to
the countryside to escape air raids. Emperor Akihito was evacuated to
Nikkō.

Long Nights

> I fall asleep,
> Fondly recalling the words of my son,
> Who told me
> Of the pleasure he takes
> In studying on long autumn nights. *(102)*

Inkstone

> Water at midnight
> Chills my fingers,
> As I wash clean
> This inkstone,
> Which I have used for so long. *(103)*

The Holly Osmanthus

> Ah, the leaves
> Of the old holly tree
> Have lost all their thorns,
> And are now
> Smooth and rounded. *(104)*

103 Title: theme for Culture Day.
    Inkstone: a device on which an inkstick is rubbed to make liquid ink.
104 Old holly osmanthus leaves tend to lose their thorns.

Meiji Shrine's Sixtieth Anniversary

> Your Majesty made so many journeys
> From far, northern Michinoku
> To the southernmost tip of Kyūshū
> In those days of your reign
> When the roads were still so rough
> and difficult!   *(105)*

1981

Sounds

> Accompanying His Highness
> As his vehicle moves on
> Along the edge of the River Akikawa
> I hear the murmur, so purifying,
> Of the waters all the way.   *(106)*

105 Meiji Shrine: see Emperor's poem *82.*
     Michinoku: see Emperor's poem *84.*
106 Title: theme for the New Year's Poetry Reading.

Rainy Season Chill

> I pick
> The fruit of the *ume*
> In the chilly garden,
> While rain continues to fall
> Unceasingly. *(107)*

Rice-planting

> I walk at evening,
> Thinking of the young rice shoots
> In the imperial fields,
> While the *unohana* in full bloom
> Shed light on the darkness. *(108)*

---

107 Rainy season: called *tsuyu* in Japanese and written using the characters for *ume* and rain because the rainy season and the ripening of the ume coincide.
    Ume: see Empress's poem *1*.

108 Imperial fields: where, each year, the Emperor plants and reaps rice.
    Unohana: or *utsugi* (*Deutzia crenata*), a deciduous shrub growing throughout Japan. The white flowers bloom in May and June.

The Autumn Equinox

At last,
The autumn equinox
Is drawing near.
How quiet is the mountain,
Capped by a wisp of white cloud!   *(109)*

Hana Yatsude

Milk-white blossoms
Of the *hana yatsude*
Have risen imperceptibly
Past dense masses of leaves
To form floral crowns.   *(110)*

110 *Hana yatsude*: meaning eight-handed, the name refers to the leaves of this
evergreen shrub of the ginseng family. The stems reach a height of two
to three metres, with leaves growing from their tops and blossoms appear-
ing in large, terminal clusters. *Fatsia japonica.*

1982

A Bridge

> Crossing a bridge,
> We arrived at a city,
> Built on the sea,
> Glittering
> In the light of March.　　　　　*(111)*

Tsukushi

> There on the hill,
> Where breezes blow gently,
> Bearing the fragrance of *ume*,
> It is chilly still—
> Too early for *tsukushi*.　　　　　*(112)*

111 Title: theme for the New Year's Poetry Reading.
　　Visiting Portopia.
　　City: refers to the 436-hectare artificial island off the port city of Kobe in Hyōgo Prefecture. The island was the site of the Kobe Port Island Exposition, or Portopia '81, held from March 20 until September 15, 1981. Under the theme 'Creation of a New Cultural City on the Sea', to which construction of the island has been devoted, the project represents the local government's experiment with an ideal future living-working environment.
112 *Tsukushi*: the edible part of the field horsetail, which appears in early spring.
　　Ume: see Empress's poem *1*.

Peonies

Midnight brings back images
Of the peonies of Sukagawa Gardens,
Spoken of by volunteer workers
I met on the grounds
During the day.   (113)

Rice-planting

The rice field
Where His Majesty planted
Each young shoot with care
Will surely bear, this year too,
A rich harvest.   (114)

113 Title: theme for the birthday of Emperor Showa.
    Sukagawa: a city, in the south of Fukushima Prefecture, famous for peonies.
    Volunteers: known as *kinrō hōshi*, they come from various areas of Japan
to clean and weed the Imperial Palace grounds and gardens. Over one
million people have volunteered their services since 1945.

Gossamer

> The rainy season is over,
> Followed by the sun's
> Scorching onslaught of heat.
> I am glad I prepared in time
> Summer kimonos of gossamer.   *(115)*

Kogarashi

> This month of November,
> When my son was born,
> Always brings back memories
> Of the cold blast of the *kogarashi*
> I heard all night long.   *(116)*

116 *Kogarashi*: literally tree-withering wind, it refers to the cold winds that blow from late autumn to early winter.

My son: Prince Fumihito, born November 30.   See Emperor's poem *159*.

1983

Island

> Reading their way through,
> Even from the waves at sea,
> They came rowing up—
> People from the Yap islands:
> A sight unforgettable! *(117)*

Island

> Blown by the island breeze,
> We saw a rocket
> Awaiting the day
> When it would join the stars
> And fly. *(118)*

---

117 Title: theme for the New Year's Poetry Reading.

    People: six men sailed 3,000 kilometres from the islands of Yap to the southern Japanese island of Okinawa in forty-seven days, using primitive navigational methods. Their canoe was displayed at the International Ocean Exposition 1975, held in Okinawa.

118 Visiting Tanegashima Space Center. See Emperor's poem *137*.

Blizzard

Is a blizzard blowing again today
On the mountains of Nepal,
Where he, who single-heartedly
Loved the mountains,
Rests in eternal sleep?   *(119)*

Sakuramochi

The *sakuramochi*
Was so delicately fragrant
That I placed a morsel
In my mouth—
Tender cherry-leaf wrapping and all!
                                            (120)

Young Bamboo

The bamboo grove
Thrives on its own.
Tall and vibrant,
With young saplings
Growing among their elders.   *(121)*

---

120 Sakuramochi: a seasonal, pale-pink, soft cake of glutinous rice, wrapped in
a young, salted cherry leaf.

In Ranjō

Ranjō, as Your Majesty wished,
Has become a green forest!
So many trees now surround
The cedars you planted
With your own hands.   (122)

Citation

Those hands
That now receive the citation
Are hands that have,
For years, fostered
The green leaves of mountains.   (123)

122 On seeing the stone memorial bearing the waka composed by Emperor
    Showa on the occasion of a tree-planting ceremony in Ranjō, Toyama
    Prefecture, in 1967. Emperor Akihito and Empress Michiko visited the spot
    in 1983. Emperor Showa's poem: Together with the people / We have
    planted cedars / With the hope / That Ranjō may become / A green hill.
123 Title: theme for Culture Day.
124 *Higurashi*: an evening cicada.
126 Title: theme for the New Year's Poetry Reading.

Higurashi

> There was a gentle look
> In my daughter's eyes
> As she listened to the *higurashi*,
> Murmuring that she loves
> The fall of evening. (*124*)

New Year's Eve

> For a long time I shall remember
> The silence of night
> Of this special year,
> When my son is away
> In another land. (*125*)

1984

Green

> Early in the morning,
> Above the green
> Of coconut trees,
> The great African sky
> Begins to burn. (*126*)

The Fountain

On hearing
A sudden burst of children's voices
I saw
The fountain in the square
Rising high.   (127)

Silk Tree Blossoms

I think of the summer day
When I climbed the slope
Of Kiire in Satsuma,
And saw, as I reached the top,
Silk trees standing there in bloom. (128)

128 Silk tree: a tree, found in Asia and the Middle East, that has flowers with
long, silky stamens.   This deciduous tree is called the *nemunoki* tree (literally,
the sleeping tree) in Japanese, because the leaves fold at night.
    Satsuma: former name for western Kagoshima, in southern Kyūshū.

Matsumushi

> Late at night,
> Mingled with the chirping
> Of the *matsumushi*,
> Echoes the sound of the guitar,
> Played, no doubt, by my son.   *(129)*

Iwashi-gumo

> Cosmos were in full bloom
> In the village we visited,
> And fleecy *iwashi-gumo*
> Floated in the sky
> At high noon.   *(130)*

129 *Matsumushi*: a member of the cricket family, the male of which produces clear, bell-like chirping sounds.
130 *Iwashi-gumo*: literally 'sardine clouds', corresponding to the English phrase 'mackerel sky'.

1985

Journey

> Those days when I stroked
> Her infant locks
> Are far in the distant past.
> My child, now growing into
>   womanhood
> Has set out on a journey.   *(131)*

Journey

> A sudden burst of colours
> Hits the window of the car
> Carrying the Prince and me,
> As we drive through a town
> With the slogan, Flowers Everywhere.
>   *(132)*

131–34 Title: theme for the New Year's Poetry Reading.
132 Visiting Yūwachō, Akita Prefecture.

Journey

> It is still early spring in Albion
> Where we have come on a journey.
> Only a few flowers
> Are blooming
> In the university town.　　　　*(133)*

Journey

> The ship of sails
> Waits in the moonlit harbour
> For the young mariners,
> About to set out on a journey,
> Seeking the sea breeze.　　　　*(134)*

133 Albion: the oldest name for Great Britain, it has been retained as the poetic name for England.
134 On the completion of the *Shin Nihon Maru*, a training ship for the Institute for Sea Training, Ministry of Transportation.

Spring Lanterns

I think of Her Majesty
In the living room
Where the spring lanterns sway,
And call to mind the *hina*
Of the festival we celebrate this eve.   *(135)*

Thunder

I recall those days
Of early childhood
When, in the countryside,
I would count the moments between
The flash of lightning and
    the thunderclap.   *(136)*

---

135 Title: theme for the birthday of the Empress Dowager.
   Hina: refers to the dolls set up for the Doll Festival on March 3. The
dolls represent the Emperor, Empress, attendants and musicians, and are
clad in ancient court attire.
136 Empress Michiko, together with part of her family, was evacuated to the
countryside during World War II.

The Sweet Osmanthus

> The sweet osmanthus
> Has bloomed—
> The sky over Tokyo
> This year
> Is refreshingly clear.   *(137)*

A Field in Winter

> Shafts of russet sunset glow
> Penetrate the windowpane,
> While out in the field,
> A wintry blast
> Blows with fury.   *(138)*

137 Osmanthus: a widely distributed genus of evergreen shrub or tree.

1986

Water

Beyond sandy stretches,
We glimpse the Sea of Okhotsk,
As we release
The young fry
Into the water of Lake Saroma.   *(139)*

Peach Blossoms

The scarlet peach blossoms
Are in flower—
Her Majesty has added another year
With the coming
Of this fine spring.   *(140)*

139 Title: theme for the New Year's Poetry Reading.
    Lake Saroma: in northeastern Hokkaidō, on the coast of the Sea of Okhotsk,
it is the third-largest lake in Japan and covers 151.7 square kilometres. A
large sandbar separates it from the Sea of Okhotsk.
140 Title: theme for the birthday of the Empress Dowager.

The following essay has been adapted from that written for the Japanese edition of Tomoshibi, *published by Fujin Gahosha in 1986, when T.I.M. the Emperor and Empress were still the Crown Prince and Princess.   The writer at the time served as Chamberlain to the Crown Prince.*

Background

> As I proceed
> Along the verandah to shinden
> The first gleam
> Of dawn appears in the sky
> of New Year's Day. *(98)*

For the Crown Prince, the year traditionally begins with special rites on New Year's Day. After rising at about 4:30 in the morning, he purifies himself and, at about 5:20, sets out for the Imperial Palace. After donning traditional formal robes, he goes to pray at the three shrines on the Palace grounds: Kashikodokoro, dedicated to Amaterasu Ōmikami; Kōreiden to the preceding emperors, empresses and members of the Imperial Family; and Shinden, to various deities. As he proceeds to the Shinden, the new year is about to dawn. Meanwhile, during the ritual, the Crown Princess goes out into the garden to pray, wishing to join the Crown Prince in spirit.

At around 6:30 in the morning, the Crown Prince returns to his residence where he celebrates the New Year with his family, but soon leaves again with the Crown Princess for the Imperial Palace. Here they accompany the Emperor and Empress when they receive New Year greetings throughout the day from Japanese and foreign government representatives. On the second day of the New Year, the Crown Prince and Princess once again go to the Imperial Palace, this time to accompany Their Majesties when they appear before the people to receive New Year wishes. And, in the early hours of the third day, the Crown Prince and Princess attend the Genshisai rites after they have purified themselves.

Throughout the year, there are 16 occasions when the Imperial Family observes traditional rites involving the offering of prayers for the peace and happiness of the nation and the veneration of the spirits of the Imperial ancestors. The Crown Prince and Princess take great care to unfailingly observe these rites. In addition, they attend ceremonial functions observed by the Emperor: the New Year's Lectures at Court, the New Year's Poetry Reading at the Imperial Court, and the Imperial Garden Party. Besides these, there are formal luncheons and banquets in honour of state and official guests. As might be expected, these guests have been increasing in recent years, and it is the role of the Crown Prince and Princess to assist the Emperor. A waka which the Crown Prince composed when he met a state guest reads:

> As we gather
> At an evening banquet
> For visitors from a foreign land,
> Layered clouds
> Flow like vermilion flags. *(102)*

The Crown Prince has travelled abroad considerably, often returning state visits as the official representative of the Emperor. The Crown Prince and Princess have paid 41 official visits overseas in the 27 years since their marriage and, blessed with good health, they have been able to carry out their busy schedule from early morning to late at night. The letters which have been received at the Crown Prince's Palace after each trip convey the deep impression made by Their Highnesses on the people of those nations. For considerations of space, I can quote only one letter, which says, in part:

'The personality and bearing of Their Highnesses gave us the impression of dignity and refinement and, at the same time, a sense of joyfulness and peace. It was wonderful that we could welcome from Japan the Crown Prince and Princess with their outstanding human qualities. That people in such an official position should make us feel once more the warmth and dignity of man is truly impressive. We were so moved by this and felt renewed.'

* * *

Among the physically handicapped
Marching in the stadium,
There is one
Accompanied by his guide dog
Trotting beside him.   *(133)*

This waka was inspired by the opening ceremony at a sports meeting for the disabled in Tottori Prefecture. The Crown Prince and Princess have always shown interest in matters relating to the disabled, and continually encourage them to seek higher goals.

They have visited all 47 prefectures, attending events, visiting facilities and institutions, and meeting people. Their Highnesses have always been particularly anxious not to overlook any of the nation's citizens, from those living on the northernmost islands of Hokkaidō to those on the southernmost islands of Okinawa. In 1963, when the future of U.S.-occupied Okinawa had still not been decided, the Crown Prince and Princess began inviting to their home the participants in an exchange programme for students from junior high schools in Japan and Okinawa. But their efforts did not end here. Following the reversion of Okinawa to Japan in 1972, they saw a need to foster understanding between the people of Japan and Okinawa, and to encourage them to share those things that are culturally important, as well as to heal the wounds caused the Okinawans by years of suffering. The Crown Prince often stressed the need to study the rich culture of which Okinawan people are so proud and, while championing their cause, he studied the history and literature of the region, and ancient *omoro* songs and ryūka poems of Okinawa under the tutelage of Dr. Shuzen Hokama. It was after a visit to the International Ocean Exposition, Okinawa, of which he was honourary president, that the Crown Prince wrote the following ryūka.

> Farmlands spread out below,
> Mount Gusuku soaring above,
> Overwhelming sorrow wells up in my mind
> With the thoughts of war. *(165)*

This ryūka is engraved on a monument on Mount Gusuku on Ie Island, half the population of which perished during World War II.

The Crown Prince and Princess hold various functions at the Crown Prince's Palace. They receive guests from abroad, including ambassadors, government emissaries, scholars and representatives of the arts.

Reflecting their interest in Japan's contribution to international cooperation, the Imperial couple have, over the past 20 years, met with the members of the Japan Overseas Cooperation Volunteers to wish them well prior to their departure. They have also gone out of their way to give words of encouragement to those volunteers they have been able to meet while travelling abroad, and it was on one such occasion that the Crown Prince composed the following waka:

> I gaze over the vast dry land,
> Together with someone
> Who came to raise vegetables
> In Senegal, a country
> Far from her homeland. *(144)*

*   *   *

When the wind blows,
Snowdrifting cherry blossom petals
For a while
Come brightly shining
Between my daughter and me. *(95)*

In this waka, the Crown Princess has very touchingly shared a happy moment on a spring day. Busy schedules make quiet moments rare for Their Highnesses and so, in order to have a little time when the family can be together before the younger ones go off to school, the day begins at 6 o'clock. As Princess Sayako remarked to a lady-in-waiting some time ago, how pleasant it is for all the members of the family to be able to share a laugh together.

While each member of the family has well-defined duties, of necessity requiring a certain amount of personal sacrifice, these duties are carefully conveyed to the children by their mother, following guidelines suggested by the Crown Prince. This enables each to respond according to age and awareness. The children have been brought up in a loving family atmosphere, and the cheerful laughter of the Princes and Princess is often heard floating through the Palace. And perhaps, as she penned the above waka, the Crown Princess was very much aware that it would not be long before the children would be leaving the nest.

When not busy with official duties, the Crown Prince devotes much of his time to research on the classification of gobies, having written 25 papers on the subject since completing his first paper in 1963. Through the exchange of papers, he has been in contact with researchers overseas, many of whom have sought reprints of his papers, and as a result of which his work is often quoted.

In 1980, the Crown Prince was elected a Foreign Member of the Linnean Society of London. Of the 50 Foreign Members prescribed by the Society's Charter, there were only two from Japan, the Crown Prince and Dr. Hiroshi Hara (1911–86), a scholar of systematic botany. Then, in 1986, the Crown Prince became an honourary member of the Society, together with H.R.H. the Prince of Wales. As coauthor, the Crown Prince has written nearly 200 articles on various kinds of goby in *The Fishes of the Japanese Archipelago*, which was completed in 1985.

While the studies of the Crown Princess are little publicized, she has continued to take interest in Japanese and English literature. Recently, although her daily schedule has become so busy that she scarcely has time to attend lectures, we often see her reading in her brief spare time. Also her fondness for music sometimes finds her, in the early morning or late at night, accompanying the Crown Prince as he plays the cello, or playing the piano or harp by herself.

I have tried to briefly describe some of the highlights in the daily life of Their Imperial Highnesses. Permeating every aspect of their routine are constant devotion to the country and the people, aspirations for better relations with other nations, and loving care for their family. They show ample concern for Their Majesties' welfare now that Emperor Hirohito and Empress Nagako have aged. They also devote great attention to the Imperial Family as a whole and to the relatives now living outside the court circle, especially those who lost their parents in childhood and those who were bereaved later in life.

Late one evening not long ago, I caught a glimpse of Their Highnesses talking together among the myriad blooming day lilies. It was a quiet and serene scene with little trace of the day's hectic schedule. When they can find a spare moment together, there is always something to which they look forward, such as the familiar horsetails, the budding white raspberry blossoms, or the Chinese quince with its autumn fruit. As each season unfolds, so, too, does their happiness.

Yasuo Shigeta
Deputy Grand Chamberlain

POEMS IN JAPANESE

Poems by
Emperor Akihito

1. Michinobe ni / Akaku irozuku / Nanakamado
   Aki koso kitsure / Yunoko no kishi ni
   道のべに赤く色づくななかまど秋こそ来つれ湯の湖の岸に

2. Itsunoma ni / Irozuki taruka / Karamatsu no
   Ha ni yawarakaku / Ame zo furi keru
   いつの間に色づきたるか落葉松の葉にやはらかく雨ぞ降りける

3. Nubatama no / Yo wa kitsure domo / Sora uzumu
   Karasu no mure no / Itsu netsukuran
   ぬばたまの夜は来つれども空埋む烏の群のいつ寝つくらむ

4. Yakushiji no / Midori no mori ni / Sobietachi
   Ake no usureshi / Sanjū no tō
   薬師寺の緑の森にそびえたち朱のうすれし三重の塔

5. Sazanami no / Ōmi no umi wa / Ame furite
   Honokani kasumu / Seta no karahashi
   さざなみの近江のうみは雨ふりてほのかに霞む瀬田の唐橋

6. Sayokaze ni / Ta no mo nagarete / Tobu hotaru
   Mizu ni utsureba / Hikaru hoshi nari
   さ夜風に田の面流れて飛ぶ螢水に映れば光る星なり

7. Haru no hi o / Ukuru karita no / Usugōri
   Awa o fukumite / Shiroku hikareri
   春の日を受くる刈田の薄氷あわをふくみて白く光れり

8. Shiohigata / Hateiru fune ni / Matsu take no
   Eda o tatete zo / Shinnen iwau
   しほ干潟泊てゐる船に松竹の枝をたててぞ新年祝ふ

9. Ōumi wa / Kaze fuki susabi / Shiranami no
   Iwa ni kudakete / Shio kemuri tatsu
   大海は風吹きすさび白波の岩にくだけて潮けむり立つ

10. Izuku yori / Chirikuru mono ka / Hanabira no
    Kaze ni fukarete / Tani watari keri
    いづくより散り来るものか花びらの風に吹かれて谷渡りけり

11. Kushimoto no / Aoki irie o / Mioroseba
    Shiranami shigeku / Ikusuji mo yoru
    串本のあをき入江を見下せば白波しげく幾すぢも寄る

12. Shizukanaru / Umi no mo ni shibashi / Nami o tate
    Oshiyose kitaru / Urokuzu no mure
    静かなる海の面にしばし波をたて押し寄せ来るうろくづの群

13. Ike no mo wa / Sakura no hana ni / Ōwarete
    Soko sumu mizu ni / Haru no ka no tatsu
    池の面は桜の花におほはれて底澄む水に春の香のたつ

14. Hisakata no / Asa no hikari ni / Nioi tachi
    Miyako no namiki / Niimidori seri
    ひさかたの朝の光ににほひたち都の並木新みどりせり

15. Misonou no / Kusaki wa aoku / Nioedomo
    Oto shizumareru / Tono no kizahashi
    御園生の草木は青くにほへども音しづまれるとののきざはし

16. Ima ichido / Aitashi to omou / Sobo-miya ni
    Uma no shiai no / Hanashi omo sezu
    今一度あひたしと思ふ祖母宮に馬の試合の話をもせず

17. Natsu no hi ni / Misono no hatake / Aomedomo
    Tareka yorokobu / Kimi masazu shite
    夏の日に御園の畠青めども誰かよろこぶ君在さずして

18. Arashio no / Unabara koete / Funade sen
    Hiroku mimawaran / Totsukuni no sama
    荒潮のうなばらこえて船出せむ広く見まはらむとつくにのさま

19. Hitoke naki / Mizuumi no mo ni / Hakuchō ichiwa
    Ware tatazumeba / Chikayorite kinu
    人気なき湖の面に白鳥一羽我たたずめば近寄りて来ぬ

20. Hezā shigeru / Areno o kuruma / Hashirasete
    Bakkurū-kō no / Yakata ni mukau
    ヘザー茂る荒野を車走らせてバックルー公の館に向かふ

21. Kogechairo no / Hezā to ishikoro no / Oka no ue ni
    Kao no ke kuroki / Hitsuji mureasobu
    こげ茶色のヘザーと石ころの岡の上に顔の毛黒き羊群遊ぶ

22. Osanaki hi / Kikishi hanashi no / Tōdai ni
    Fune chikazukinu / Nami yokogirite
    幼き日聞きし話の灯台に船近づきぬ波よこ切りて

23. Kusamura ni / Tamago idakite / Yasumu kamo
    Hito chikazuku mo / Ugokazari keri
    草むらに卵いだきてやすむ鴨人近づくも動かざりけり

24. Yoru fukete / Machi o arukeba / Hodō no ue wa
    Koyoi o akasu / Hitobito ni umaru
    夜ふけて街を歩けば歩道の上はこよひを明かす人々にうまる

25. Machi o izureba / Kusa madaranaru / Oka mata oka
    Iteru hi no moto / Kuruma hashirasu
    街をいづれば草まだらなる丘また丘い照る日のもと車走らす

26. Wakaki kimi no / Unten shitamau / Jidōsha wa
    Hi no moruru hayashi / Baba e to isogu
    若き君の運転し給ふ自動車は日のもるる林馬場へと急ぐ

27. Hayashi ari / Hara aru nagame ni / Miiri tsutsu
    Autobān nite / Toki tatsu o shirazu
    林あり原あるながめに見入りつつアウトバーンにて時たつを知らず

28. Ishi ōku / Ki no ouru naki / Takahara wa
    Kasumi no hate ni / Tsuzuki yukitari
    石おほく木の生ふるなき高原は霞のはてに続き行きたり

29. Ikujūri / Hashiredo keshiki wa / Kawari kozu
    Midori no iro naki / Areno wa tsuzuku
    幾十里走れど景色は変り来ず緑の色なき荒野は続く

30. Miwatasu kagiri / Tsuzuku areno ni / Kamoshika no
    Asobu o nagame / Shibashi tatazumu
    見わたすかぎり続く荒野にかもしかの遊ぶを眺めしばしたたずむ

31. Hantoshi no / Tabi yori kaeri / Ima nozomu
    Kumo no aima no / Hinomoto no tsuchi
    半年の旅より帰りいま望む雲の合間の日の本の土

32. Kokukoku ni / Ōkiku mie kuru / Bokoku no machi
    Sōjūshitsu yori / Akazu nagamenu
    刻々に大きく見え来る母国の街操縦室よりあかず眺めぬ

33. Tabiji yori / Kaerite yadoru / Karuizawa
    Irozuku hayashi wa / Bokoku no ka ni mitsu
    旅路より帰りて宿る軽井沢色づく林は母国の香にみつ

34. Igirisu no / Taikanshiki ni / Ikishi yori
    Kono hitotose wa / Haya sugisarinu
    イギリスの戴冠式に行きしよりこの一年は早や過ぎ去りぬ

35. Imagoro wa / Sazo utsukushikaran to / Ori ni fure
    Omoi izuruwa / Rondon no shoka
    今頃はさぞ美しからむと折にふれ思ひ出づるはロンドンの初夏

36. Sumitōru / Izumi no soko wa / Koke aomi
    Wakiizuru mizu / Oto naku nagaru
    すみとほる泉の底は苔青みわき出づる水音なく流る

37. Minemine o / Koete hirogaru / Akizora wa
    Oku fukaku shite / Sumi watari keri
    峯々を越えてひろがる秋空は奥深くしてすみわたりけり

38. Seseragi o / Ōishi kōri / Tokeyukite
    Iwabashiru mizu / Tagichi sometari
    せせらぎをおほひし氷とけゆきて石ばしる水たぎちそめたり

39. Tomoshibi no / Shizukani moyuru / Shinkaden
    Koto hajiki utau / Koe hikuku hibiku
    ともしびの静かにもゆる神嘉殿琴はじきうたふ声ひくく響く

40. Niimidori / Moyuru satsuki no / Misonou ni
    Wakaba kamurite / Taruru shirafuji
    新緑萌ゆる五月の御園生に若葉かむりて垂るる白藤

41. Damuzukuri no / Eiga mishi ato / Koko ni kite
    Kono me nite mitsutsu / Tōji o shinobu
    ダム作りの映画見し後ここに来てこの目にて見つつ当時をしのぶ

161

42. Kazu ōki / Giseisha ideshi / Damu no kabe
     Yamaai ni takaku / Sobie tachitari

    数多き犠牲者出でしダムの壁山間に高くそびえたちたり

43. Ōzora wa / Ken'un hitotsu / Tadayoeri
     Komakaki ito o / Ikue mo hikite

    大空は巻雲ひとつただよへり細かき糸をいく重もひきて

44. Hakushu waki / Afuganisutan no hata / Arawarenu
     Ajia taikai / Koko ni hajimaru

    拍手わきアフガニスタンの旗現れぬアジア大会ここに始まる

45. Seika kie / Taimatsu inarabu / Daikyōgijō
     'Hotaru no hikari' / Awaku nagaruru

    聖火消えたいまつ居ならぶ大競技場「ほたるの光」淡く流るる

46. Sutando no / Hakushu ni kotae / Sariyuku wa
     Omoi omoi ni / Te o furikaesu

    スタンドの拍手にこたへ去り行くは思ひ思ひに手を振り返す

47. Kōgai ni / Izureba kigi no / Asamidori
     Honshū no yama / Hashiru kokochisu

    郊外に出づれば木々の浅みどり本州の山走る心地す

48. Ame keburu / Yama koekureba / Yamaai no
     Tankō no machi / Ie komiaeri

    雨けぶる山越えくれば山間の炭坑の町家こみあへり

49. Sukashiyuri / Hamanasu shigeru / Sakyū tsuzuki
     Ohōtsuku no umi / Shizukeku shiroshi

    すかしゆりはまなす茂る砂丘つづきオホーツクの海静けく白し

50. Katarai o / Kasane yukitsutsu / Ki ga tsukinu
     Ware no kokoro ni / Hirakitaru mado

    語らひを重ねゆきつつ気がつきぬわれのこころに開きたる窓

162

51. Fuyubi sasu / Mokkoku no ha wa / Shiroku teri
    Kaze ni yuragite / Mado ni utsureri
    冬日さす木斛の葉は白く光り風にゆらぎて窓にうつれり

52. Aoguroku / Takaku shigereru / Sugi no ki no
    Eda miagetsutsu / Sandō susumu
    青黒く高く茂れる杉の木の枝見上げつつ参道すすむ

53. Ki ni kageru / Sandō o kite / Kakiuchi nari
    Atarashiki miya ni / Asahi kagayaku
    木にかげる参道を来て垣内なり新しき宮に朝日かがやく

54. Hiru fukaki / Hikari furishiku / Narabayashi
    Ochiba no ue wa / Hi no hadarenari
    昼ふかき光降りしく楢林落葉の上は日のはだれなり

55. Shirakaba no / Tsubomi tareyuki / Kozue no ue
    Haru to naritaru / Sora o chiribamu
    白樺のつぼみたれゆき梢の上春となりたる空をちりばむ

56. Mirugoto ni / Wakame nobiyuku / Shirakaba ni
    Haru fukamaruo / Me ni shimi ajiwau
    見るごとに若芽のびゆく白樺に春深まるを目にしみ味はふ

57. Akatsuchi no / Yamahara tsuzuku / Michi no hate
    Kuruma chikazuku / Peruseporisu no hashira
    赤土の山原続く道のはて車近づくペルセポリスの柱

58. Miharukasu / Kusahara no naka / Akashiya no
    Kozue tairani / Mabarani ouru
    見はるかす草原の中アカシヤの梢平らにまばらに生ふる

59. Akashiya no / Edaeda ni sagaru / Kotori no su
    Afurika ni aru o / Minishimi omou
    アカシヤの枝々にさがる小鳥の巣アフリカにあるを身にしみおもふ

60. Kuroki mono / Chikayoru ni tsure / Katachi nasu
    Savanna no naka no / Orikkusu no mure
    黒きもの近寄るにつれ形なすサヴァンナの中のオリックスの群

61. Hibi nurumi / Hibi tokeyukite / Yuki no shita ni
    Nururu niitsuchi / Kyō arawaretsu
    日日温み日日とけゆきて雪の下にぬるる新土今日現はれつ

62. Funaberi ni / Miiru asaumi no / Konjō o
    Sōdagatsuo no / Tsuranuki hashiru
    舷に見入る朝海の紺青をそうだがつをのつらぬき走る

63. Afurika no / Ōki kusahara / Tsuzuku naka o
    Orikkusu oi / Kagamite susumu
    アフリカの大き草原つづくなかをオリックス追ひかがみて進む

64. Atsumetaru / Washi nagametsutsu / Sorezore no
    Sukareshi sube o / Omoi katarau
    蒐めたる和紙ながめつつそれぞれの漉かれしすべをおもひ語らふ

65. Kaze fukite / Obana midaruru / Takahara ni
    Natsu ni mizarishi / Hana saki niou
    風吹きて尾花乱るる高原に夏に見ざりし花咲き匂ふ

66. Tori ichiwa / Tobitachi izuru / Fuyubayashi
    Ake ni tanabiku / Kumo o hatateni
    鳥一羽飛び立ち出づる冬林朱にたなびく雲をはたてに

67. Mioroseba / Mori ni tsugu mori / Hitosuji no
    Mekon no nagare / Shirobikari seri
    見下せば森につぐ森一すぢのメコンの流れ白光りせり

68. Taikoku no / Kimi to kisaki to / Tsuredachite
    Warera mukau wa / Byōzoku no buraku
    タイ国の君と后とつれ立ちて我等向かふは苗族の部落

164

69. Byōzoku no / Buraku ni mukau / Yamamichi ni
    Imo ga mitsukeshi / Tsurifune no hana
    苗族の部落に向かふ山道に妹が見つけしつりふねの花

70. Michinobe no / Yamahana mitsutsu / Oriyukeba
    Ki no yakiharawareshi / Buraku ni idenu
    道の辺の山花見つつ下りゆけば木の焼きはらはれし部落に出でぬ

71. Kodomora no / Asobi tawamururu / Koe no naka
    Hitokiwa takashi / Haha o yobu ako
    子供等の遊びたはむるる声のなかひときは高し母を呼ぶ吾子

72. Osanaki hi / Manabi no sono e / Kayou toki
    Kikishi yamabato / Ako mo kikuran
    幼き日学びの園へ通ふとき聞きし山鳩吾子も聞くらむ

73. Hiroshiba o / Umuru hitomure / Hata mochite
    Furu oto kikoyu / Kyōno yoki hi o
    広芝をうむる人群旗持ちて振る音聞ゆ今日のよき日を

74. Reizen ni / Shibashi no toki o / Suwari oreba
    Mimi ni ukabinu / Arishi hi no koe
    霊前にしばしの時を座り居れば耳に浮かびぬありし日の声

75. Garasuheki ni / Umishi tamago o / Kawariaite
    Oya no tirapia / Mamori tsuzukeori
    ガラス壁に産みし卵をかはりあひて親のティラピア守り続けをり

76. Andesu no / Tanima o kezuru / Rimaku-gawa
    Soi nobori yuku / Jidōsha-michi wa
    アンデスの谷間をけづるリマク川沿ひのぼりゆく自動車道は

77. Kono mizu no / Nagaruru saki wa / Amazon kakō
    Te o hitashi miru ni / Hono hiyayakeshi
    この水の流るる先はアマゾン河口手をひたしみるにほのひややけし

78. Osanabi no / Mimi ni shitashimishi / Minami jūji
    Ware wa minikeri / Perū no yozora ni

    幼な日の耳にしたしみし南十字我は見にけりペルーの夜空に

79. Haru o matsu / Tsubomi no fusa wa / Sodachitsutsu
    Sawani tareori / Hannoki no kozue

    春を待つつぼみのふさは育ちつつさにたれをりはんのきのこずゑ

80. Shiroato wa / Kinaru hanabana / Sakimiteri
    Nan no hana kato / Omoitsutsu noboru

    城跡は黄なる花々咲き満てり何の花かと思ひつつのぼる

81. Asa no hi ni / Michibe no yuki wa / Kagayakite
    Hareshi sora no moto / Bankoku hakurankai hiraku

    朝の日に道辺の雪は輝きて晴れし空の下万国博覧会開く

82. Sumerogi no / Kizuki tamaishi / Ishizue ni
    Bankokuhaku wa / Hana hirakitari

    すめろぎの築きたまひしいしずゑに万国博は花開きたり

83. Mizuumi ni / Sosogu ogawa o / Nobori koshi
    Ichibi no masu wa / Hashishita ni ikou

    湖に注ぐ小川を上り来し一尾の鱒は橋下にいこふ

84. Wara o yaku / Kemuri nagaruru / Ta no tsuzuki
    Hi wa kureyukeri / Michinoku no sato

    藁を焼く煙流るる田の続き日は暮れ行けり陸奥の里

85. Ashinami o / Soroe irikuru / Shinshōsha
    Michinoku no kyōgijō / Hakushu nariwataru

    足並を揃へ入り来る身障者陸奥の競技場拍手鳴り渡る

86. Osanaki hi / Kunimasu sumuto / Shirishi umi
    Ima tōri yuku / Kishibe shizukeshi

    幼き日国鱒住むと知りし湖いま通り行く岸辺静けし

87. Kishi no iwa ni / Mizu karoyakani / Yosekaesu
    Momiji irodoru / Ame no Tazawako
    岸の岩に水軽やかに寄せ返す紅葉彩る雨の田沢湖

88. Taimatsu no / Hi ni terasarete / Sunoko no ue
    Ho o susumeyuku / Inishie omoite
    松明の火に照らされてすのこの上歩を進め行く古思ひて

89. Niiname no / Matsuri hajimarinu / Shinkaden
    Hichiriki no oto / Shizukani nagaru
    新嘗の祭始まりぬ神嘉殿ひちりきの音静かに流る

90. Hichiriki no / Oto to awasete / Utau koe
    Shijima no naka ni / Hikuku tayutou
    ひちりきの音と合せて歌ふ声しじまの中に低くたゆたふ

91. Utagoe no / Shirabe takarakani / Nariyukeri
    Ware wa mitsumuru / Chiisaki tomoshibi
    歌声の調べ高らかになりゆけり我は見つむる小さきともしび

92. Utau koe / Shizumarite kikoyu / Kono toki ni
    Tsugebumi yomasu / Ōdokanaru mikoe
    歌ふ声静まりて聞ゆこの時に告文読ますおほどかなる御声

93. Hai o oe / Modorite haberu / Shibaraku o
    Sanretsu no hito no / Kutsuoto shigeshi
    拝を終へ戻りて侍るしばらくを参列の人の靴音繁し

94. Yūbe no gi / Koko ni owarinu / Utagoe no
    Kasukani hibiku / Modori yuku michi
    夕べの儀ここに終りぬ歌声のかすかに響く戻りゆく道

95. Toridori no / Gakki ni komete / Hiku 'Ieji'
    Narihibikitari / Shinshōsha no ie
    とりどりの楽器にこめて弾く「家路」鳴り響きたり身障者の家

167

96. Uchitsuzuku / Tsuchi no yamanami ni / Ikusuji mo
    Hito to kemono no / Tōri koshi michi
    うちつづく土の山なみに幾筋も人とけものの通りこし道

97. Tsuburanaru / Manako korashite / Wako wa iu
    Shuro no ha no e ni / Toge no arishito
    つぶらなるまなここらして吾子は言ふしゅろの葉の柄にとげのありしと

98. Shinden e / Sunoko no ue o / Susumiyuku
    Toshi no hajime no / Sora shirami somu
    神殿へすのこの上をすすみ行く年の始の空白み初む

99. Ōzora ni / Hanabi no kemuri / Nagareyuku
    Kokutai sukī no / Maku hirakitari
    大空に花火の煙流れ行く国体スキーの幕開きたり

100. Jūgonen / Sugikoshi tsukihi no / Hayakikana
     Wako wa nobori yuku / Ki no tarappu o
     十五年過ぎこし月日の早きかな吾子は上り行く機のタラップを

101. Kamiasobi no / Uta nagaruru naka / Tsugebumi no
     Mikoe kikoe ku / Niiname no yoru
     神あそびの歌流るるなか告文の御声聞え来新嘗の夜

102. Totsukuni no / Marebito to tsudou / Yo no utage
     Toyohatagumo wa / Ake ni tanabiku
     とつくにのまれ人と集ふ夜の宴豊幡雲は朱にたなびく

103. Totsukuni no / Ware o mukauru / Kora no koe
     Hibiki watareri / 'Kōjō no tsuki'
     外国の我を迎ふる子等の声響き渡れり「荒城の月」

104. Akaki hana / Shakunage no ki wa / Arawarenu
     Kuruma wa susumu / Buruchoki no yama
     赤き花しやくなげの木は現れぬ車は進むブルチョキの山

168

105. Ikusabi ni / Yaki tsukusareshi / Mabunigaoka
Misotose o hete / Ima nobori yuku
戦火に焼き尽くされし摩文仁が岡みそとせを経て今登り行く

106. Tatakai ni / Ikuta no inochi o / Ubaitaru
Ido e no michi ni / Kigi oishigeru
戦ひに幾多の命を奪ひたる井戸への道に木々生ひ茂る

107. Tatakai no / Owarite koko ni / Sanjūnen
Kurikaeshi omowan / Kono oka no koto
戦ひの終りてここに三十年くりかへし思はむこの岡のこと

108. Misotose no / Rekishi nagaretari / Mabuni no saka
Tairakeki yo ni omou / Inochi tōtoshi
みそとせの歴史流れたり摩文仁の坂平らけき世に思ふ命たふとし

109. Totsukuni no / Kimi to nori izuru / Umi no ue
Kuroki iwayama ni / Tsuki michi noboru
外国の君と乗り出づる海の上黒き岩山に月満ち上る

110. Sumitōru / Kishibe ni tachite / Oki mireba
Akaba no umi ni / Ōbune wa mitsu
すみとほる岸辺に立ちて沖見ればアカバの海に大船は満つ

111. Ashizuri no / Misaki harukeku / Kuroshio no
Umi hirogareri / Sayani hikarite
足摺の岬はるけく黒潮の海広がれりさやに光りて

112. Namerakani / Fune susumiyuku / Mutsu no umi
Miokuru hito no / Koe ato ni shite
なめらかに船進み行くむつの海見送る人の声後にして

113. Yoritsudou / Shinshō no senshu to / Tomoni miru
Hitoe no asunaro / Shibafu ni hirogoru
寄り集ふ身障の選手と共に見る人絵のあすなろ芝生に広ごる

169

114. Yasuragini / Omo wa michitari / Tarachine no
Haha no manazashi / Ukete nemuru ko
やすらぎに面はみちたりたらちねの母のまなざし受けて眠る子

115. Toshioite / Hakuchō no tou / Umi mashinu
Tairakeki yo no / Akashi tozo omou
年おひて白鳥の訪ふ湖増しぬたひらけき世の徴とぞおもふ

116. Hinomoto no / Chi o hiku hito no / Umetsukusu
Shiki wa takanaru / Burajiru no sora
日の本の血を引く人の埋め尽す式は高鳴るブラジルの空

117. Totsukuni ni / Chi o wakeshi hito to / Yoritsudoi
Tomoni kaerimiru / Shichijūnen no nagare
外国に血を分けし人と寄り集ひ共に顧みる七十年の流れ

118. Sangaoka no / Moto no umibe wa / Awadachite
Michishio ni nori / Kusafugu wa yosu
三ヶ岡の下の海辺は泡立ちて満潮に乗りくさふぐは寄す

119. Suchāba no / Aki no yūgure / Chikazukinu
Tsuchi no hatake ni / Hito no kage nashi
スチャーバの秋の夕暮近づきぬ土の畑に人の影なし

120. Fukamiyuku / Aki no kokkai / Nami tachite
Tsutsumi no kage ni / Kurage tadayou
深みゆく秋の黒海波立ちて堤の陰にくらげただよふ

121. Yotose nimo / Haya chikazukinu / Nakijin no
Akaki sakura no / Hana o mishi yori
四年にもはや近づきぬ今帰仁のあかき桜の花を見しより

122. Uerarete / Toshi nao asaki / Mokuren no
Chiisaki kozue ni / Sakisomeshi hana
植ゑられて年なほあさき木蓮の小さき梢に咲きそめし花

170

123. Momotose o / Iwau tsudoi ni / Sendatsu no
Isao kaerimi / Kano miyo o omou

百年を祝ふ集ひに先達の功かへりみ彼の御代を思ふ

124. Kurumaisu ni / Norite pianika / Fuku kora no
Oto narihibiku / Aki no kōtei

車椅子に乗りてピアニカ吹く子らの音鳴り響く秋の校庭

125. Unariyuku / Kurumaisu no oto / Kishiru oto
Rōkyūjō wa / Seien ni mitsu

うなりゆく車椅子の音きしる音籠球場は声援に満つ

126. Seinen ni / Naritaru wako to / Tomoni mukau
Miyai no hatsuzora / Harewataritari

成年に成りたる吾子と共に向かふ宮居の初空晴れ渡りたり

127. Sakuradai no / Nigiwau umi ni / Nasantote
Sodateshi kodai / Mure oyogi izu

桜鯛のにぎはふ海になさむとてそだてし小鯛群れおよぎ出づ

128. Shasō yori / Harukeku nozomu / Okuhamanako
Tōmei no hashi / Sayakani ukabu

車窓よりはるけく望む奥浜名湖東名の橋清かに浮かぶ

129. Chichigimi to / Hahagimi to ideshi / Haru no umi
Kaze fuku naka o / Tateishi ni mukau

父君と母君と出でし春の海風吹く中を立石に向かふ

130. Kanata yori / Kanū wa kawa no mo / Suberi kuru
Kai karoyakani / Mizu o kakitsutsu

彼方よりカヌーは川の面滑り来るかい軽やかに水をかきつつ

131. Shijimi toru / Kobune kitarite / Mawariyuku
Hitoyo sugoshishi / Shinjiko no asa

しじみ取る小舟来りてまはり行く一夜過ごしし宍道湖の朝

171

132. Shōgai o / Norikoe tsudou / Senshura no
　　　 Yorokobi ni fure / Kyōgi mimamoru
　　　 障害を乗り越え集ふ選手らの喜びに触れ競技見守る

133. Shinshō no / Hitobito susumu / Kyōgijō
　　　 Mōdōken mo / Soi ayumiyuku
　　　 身障の人々すすむ競技場盲導犬も添ひあゆみ行く

134. Kakuchi yori / Tsudoishi hito to / Noriidete
　　　 Kodai hanateri / Kasumi no umi ni
　　　 各地より集ひし人と乗り出でて小鯛放てり香住の海に

135. Minami naru / Iriomotejima ni / Toreshi haze
　　　 Kuroobihaze to / Nazuke shirushinu
　　　 南なる西表島にとれしはぜくろおびはぜと名付け記しぬ

136. Tsugitsugi to / Atarashiki haze / Miidaseru
　　　 Minami no shima no / Ashita o omou
　　　 次々と新しきはぜ見出せる南の島のあしたを思ふ

137. Ōzora ni / Uchiage semaru / Roketto wa
　　　 Shima no minami no / Hate ni tachitari
　　　 大空に打上げせまるロケットは島の南の果に立ちたり

138. Kurumaisu no / Rōkyūjō ni / Senshura wa
　　　 Te o fureaite / Kachishi o ajiwau
　　　 車椅子の籠球場に選手等は手を触れ合ひて勝ちしを味はふ

139. Kusagusa no / Inochi mamorikoshi / Iriomote no
　　　 Shima wa midori ni / Michite tachitari
　　　 種々の生命守り来し西表の島は緑に満ちて立ちたり

140. Chigirishi wa / Nijūgonen no / Mukashi nari
　　　 Mabuta ni ukabu / Hana ni michishi hi
　　　 契りしは二十五年の昔なりまぶたに浮かぶ花に満ちし日

172

141. Oranda no / Kimi mo kuwawaru / Berugī no
     Miyai no yoru wa / Haya fukeyukinu
     オランダの君も加はるベルギーの宮居の夜ははや更けゆきぬ

142. Aoki umi / Kawakishi daichi o / Koeyukite
     Ki wa chikazukinu / Dakāru kūkō
     青き海乾きし大地を越えゆきて機は近づきぬダカール空港

143. Amatanaru / Dorei okurishi / Goretō ni
     Hito no rekishi no / Nagare o omou
     あまたなる奴隷送りしゴレ島に人の歴史の流れを思ふ

144. Senegaru no / Yasai tsukuri ni / Harukekumo
     Koshi hito to miru / Kawakishi daichi
     セネガルの野菜つくりにはるけくも来し人と見る乾きし大地

145. Tsurube nite / Kumiageshi mizu / Senegaru no
     Kawakishi hatake no / Tsuchi ni shimiiru
     つるべにてくみ上げし水セネガルの乾きし畑の土にしみ入る

146. Hinomoto no / Hito no aseshite / Tsukuritaru
     Matadī no hashi / Dakuryū no ue ni
     日の本の人の汗してつくりたるマタディの橋濁流の上に

147. Nai ni yoru / Yamahada eguru / Jisuberi no
     Ato namanamashi / Terebi wa utsusu
     なゐによる山膚ゑぐる地滑りの跡生々しテレビは写す

148. Tabi no asa no / Mado yori mireba / Iwatesan
     Mamukai ni tatsu / Fumoto momiji ni
     旅の朝の窓より見れば岩手山真向かひに立つふもと紅葉に

149. Shōnen no / Otozureshi yori / Yonhyakunen
     Eru-esukoriaru o / Sora yori nozomu
     少年の訪れしより四百年エル・エスコリアルを空より望む

173

150. Sora meguru / Esukoriaru ni / Hitobito wa
Hata o nabikase / Wagaki o mukau

空めぐるエスコリアルに人々は旗をなびかせ我が機を迎ふ

151. Upusara ni / Fumi mite shinobu / Totsukuni to
Waga kunibito no / Majiwarishi ato

ウブサラに文見てしのぶ外国と我が国人の交はりしあと

152. Fiyorudo no / Kishi no murabito / Tsudou naka
Waga kunibito mo / Tazune kitarinu

フィヨルドの岸の村人集ふ中我が国人もたづね来りぬ

153. Noruuē no / Kimi to tazunuru / Kōen ni
Natsu no hi yawaku / Furisosogi keri

ノルウェーの君とたづぬる公園に夏の日やはく降りそそぎけり

154. Banrai no / Hakushu wakitatsu / Kyōgijō
Tatakai oeshi / Senshu irikuru

万雷の拍手わき立つ競技場戦ひ終へし選手入り来る

155. Sangosō no / Kuki irozukite / Sawani tatsu
Yūkaze samuki / Notoroko no kishi

さんごさうの茎色づきてさはに立つ夕風寒き能取湖の岸

156. Totsukuni no / Manabi no sono ni / Futatose o
Sugoshishi wako wa / Ima kaeri kuru

外国の学びの園にふたとせを過しし吾子は今帰り来る

157. Kyōgijō no / Hakushu no naka o / Seriaite
Kurumaisu marason no / Senshu irikinu

競技場の拍手の中を競り合ひて車椅子マラソンの選手入り来ぬ

158. Uerareshi / Matsu wa hisa ni / Umoretsutsu
Misotose tachite / Hayashi ni sodachinu

植ゑられし松は飛砂に埋もれつつみそとせたちて林に育ちぬ

159. Seinen ni / Naritaru wako wa / Akesomeshi
Ashita tachikeri / Ise ni mukaite
成年になりたる吾子は明け初めし朝立ちけり伊勢に向ひて

160. Totsukuni no / Tabi yori kaeri / Hinomoto no
Yutakeki mizu no / Sachi o omoinu
外国の旅より帰り日の本の豊けき水の幸を思ひぬ

161. Hana yu ushagiyun / Fitu shiranu tamashii
Ikusa neranu yuyu / Chimu ni nigati
花よおしやげゆん人知らぬ魂戦ないらぬ世よ肝に願て

162. Fusakeyuru kikusa / Miguru ikusaatu
Kurikaishi gaishi / Umui kakiti
ふさかいゆる木草めぐる戦跡くり返し返し思ひかけて

163. Danjukariyushi nu / Utagui nu fibichi
Miukuru waregau / Mi nidu nukuru
だんじよかれよしの歌声の響見送る笑顔目にど残る

164. Danjukariyushi nu / Uta ya wachagatan
Yūna sachuru shima / Chimu ni nukuti
だんじよかれよしの歌や湧上がたんゆうな咲きゆる島肝に残て

165. Firugayuru hataki / Tachuru gusikuyama
Chimu nu shinubaranu / Ikusayu nu kutu
広がゆる畑立ちゆる城山肝のしのばらぬ戦世の事

166. Nachijin nu gusiku / Jō nu uchi iriba
Sacharu sakurabana / Bin ni sumiti
今帰仁の城門の内入れば咲きやる桜花紅に染めて

175

Poems by
Empress Michiko

1. Tsubarakani / Sakisomeshi ume / Aogitsutsu
   Yasashiki haru no / Sora ni mamukau

   つばらかに咲きそめし梅仰ぎつつ優しき春の空に真むかふ

2. Misonou o / Idemasu kimi ga / Michimichi ni
   Mebuki sugashi mo / Haru no wakakusa

   御苑生をいでます君が道みちに芽吹き清しも春の若草

3. Azukareru / Takara nimo nite / Arutoki wa
   Wako nagara kaina / Osoretsutsu idaku

   あづかれる宝にも似てあるときは吾子ながらかひな畏れつつ抱く

4. Harokeku mo / Umi koete koshi / Samidori no
   Ōtani watari / Shimme tsuketari

   はろけくも海越えて来しさ緑の大谷渡り新芽つけたり

5. Atarashiki / Takaki inochi no / Ayumi koko ni
   Hajimemasan ka / On-kutsu mairasu

   新しき貴きいのちの歩みここにはじめまさむか御靴まゐらす

176

6. Futo samete / Tsuchi no ka kouru / Haru chikaki
   Hitoyo shimoba no / Chiru o kikitsutsu
   ふと覚めて土の香恋ふる春近き一夜霜葉の散るを聞きつつ

7. Izuku yori / Michi koshi mono ka / Konjō no
   Sora uzume haru no / Hikari no ushio
   いづくより満ち来しものか紺青の空埋め春の光のうしほ

8. Wako tōku / Oki koshi tabi no / Haha no hi ni
   Haha naki kora no / Utai kureshi uta
   吾子遠く置き来し旅の母の日に母なき子らの歌ひくれし歌

9. Kōunki / Wakaki ga fumite / Sōgen no
   Tsuchi wa rupinasu no / Hana o maze yuku
   耕耘機若きが踏みて草原の土はルピナスの花をまぜゆく

10. Shiratama wa / Kusagusa no iro / Himuru naka
    Sayanishi tamotsu / Unabara no iro
    白珠はくさぐさの色秘むる中さやにしたもつ海原のいろ

11. Maganashiku / Hi o terikaesu / Tenjishi no
    Moji utaretsutsu / Kage o nashi yuku
    まがなしく日を照りかへす点字紙の文字打たれつつ影をなしゆく

12. Kono oka ni / Kusa moyuru toki / Chikami kamo
    Tsuchi no hogure ni / Kigisu ikoeru
    この丘に草萌ゆるとき近みかも土のほぐれにきぎすいこへる

13. Suiheisen / Yawaragi fufumi / Sosogi kuru
    Kono kuroshio no / Umi mitasu toki
    水平線やはらぎふふみそそぎ来るこの黒潮の海満たすとき

14. Areshi yori / Mika o sugushishi / Midorigo ni
    Mizumizu to shite / Soi kitaru mono
    生れしより三日を過ぐししみどり児に瑞みづとして添ひきたるもの

15. Shōnen no / Koe ni mono iu / Ko to narite
    Honokani tsuchi no / Ka mo mochi kaeru
    少年の声にものいふ子となりてほのかに土の香も持ちかへる

16. Kono hibi o / Hatanami no naka / Tabi yukasu
    Ōmi hohoemi / Shinobi sugoshinu
    この日々を旗波の中旅ゆかすおほみほほ笑みしのび過ごしぬ

17. Tenaraeru / Kami no yohaku ni / Umi to kaku
    Ariso ni kimi ga / Uo torasu hi o
    手習へる紙の余白に海と書く荒磯に君が魚獲らす日を

18. Tadoki naku / Kimi naki o omou / Kokoro tokare
    Atatamerarete / Arishi hibi wamo
    たどきなく君なきを思ふ心解かれあたためられてありし日日はも

19. Arishi hi no / Tsuzuku gani futo / Omohoyuru
    Kono satsukibi o / Kimi wa imasazu
    ありし日の続くがにふと思ほゆるこの五月日を君はいまさず

20. Tera-rossha / Tsuzukeru hate no / Kanashimo yo
    Amazon wa nagare / Harakara no sumu
    赤色土つづける果ての愛しもよアマゾンは流れ同胞の棲む

21. Moro no te o / Sora ni hiraki te / Hana-fubuki
    Toraen to suru / Ko mo haru ni mau
    双の手を空に開きて花吹雪とらへむとする子も春に舞ふ

22. Tokō-michi no / Nagate magirawashi / Kora no hamu
    Amashiba no ha no / Wakaki amazusa
    登校道の長手まぎらはし子らの食むアマシバの葉の稚き甘酸さ

23. Ikukōnen / Taiko no hikari / Ima sashite
    Chikyū wa haru o / Totonouru daichi
    幾光年太古の光いまさして地球は春をととのふる大地

24. Sachi mune ni / Aogi matsureri / Ōkimi no
    Niitakadono ni / Tatase tamaeru

幸むねに仰ぎまつれり大君の新高殿に立たせ給へる

25. Heya nuchi ni / Yūbe no hikari / Oyobi kinu
    Hanabira no goto / Wako wa nemurite

部屋ぬちに夕べの光および来ぬ花びらのごと吾子は眠りて

26. Sakyū wamo / Ikeru ga gotoku / Ugokishi to
    Wakaki gakuto wa / Tōki me ni iu

砂丘はも生けるが如く動きしと若き学徒は遠き目に云ふ

27. Osoaki no / Kareshiba majiru / Hironohara
    Kage fumi asobu / Osanago to kite

おそ秋の枯芝まじる広野原影ふみ遊ぶ幼な子と来て

28. Niikusa no / Michi ni tomadou / Shibaraku o
    Mikoe rengyō no / Hana saku atari

にひ草の道にとまどふしばらくをみ声れんげうの花咲くあたり

29. Furiaogu / Kano ōzora no / Asamidori
    Kakaru kokoro to / Oboshi meshiken

ふり仰ぐかの大空のあさみどりかかる心と懇し召しけむ

30. Harukanaru / Toi no misaki no / Yasei-uma
    Tategami wa shio no / Ka o motsuran ka

はるかなる都井の岬の野生馬たてがみは潮の香を持つらむか

31. Asobi tsukare / Kaeri koshi ko no / Unaigami
    Hagi no kobana no / Sokokoko ni chiru

遊びつかれ帰り来し子のうなゐ髪萩の小花のそこここに散る

32. Chabatake no / Shiroki kobana no / Tsutsumashimo
    Teriha no kageri / Ukete hanasaku

茶畑の白き小花のつつましも照り葉のかげり受けて花咲く

33. Ie ni matsu / Wako mitari arite / Koyuki furu
    Furusato no kuni ni / Kaeri kitarinu
    家に待つ吾子みたりありて粉雪降るふるさとの国に帰りきたりぬ

34. Wakaki mami / Sumase hitoyo no / Waza to nasu
    Kakumaku-ishoku o / Kimi wa katarishi
    若きまみ澄ませ一生の業となす角膜移植を君は語りし

35. Kaku nurete / Izokura to inoru / Sarani sarani
    Hitanurete kimira / Yuki tamaishi ka
    かく濡れて遺族らと祈る更にさらにひたぬれて君ら逝き給ひしか

36. Bāmian no / Tsuki honoakaku / Sekibutsu wa
    Mikao sogarete / Tachi tamai keri
    バーミアンの月ほのあかく石仏は御貌削がれて立ち給ひけり

37. Fuyuyama no / Shizumoru juhyō / Me ni tatsu to
    Samuyo ni wako no / Futo katari kaku
    冬山の静もる樹氷目に顕つと寒夜に吾子のふと語りかく

38. Takahara no / Hana midare saku / Yamamichi ni
    Hitora shitashi mo / Yobikawashitsutsu
    高原の花みだれ咲く山道に人ら親しも呼びかはしつつ

39. Ikanaran / Ōji ya nemuri / Imashiken
    Yami ni seishuku no / Zu aru sekikaku
    いかならむ皇子や眠りいましけむ闇に星宿の図ある石槨

40. Kuroshio no / Hikuki toyomi ni / Shinsei no
    Shima nari to tsugu / Muteki narishito
    黒潮の低きとよみに新世の島なりと告ぐ霧笛鳴りしと

41. Ame hageshiku / Sosogu Mabuni no / Oka no be ni
    Kizutsukishi mono / Amari ni ōku
    雨激しくそそぐ摩文仁の岡の辺に傷つきしものあまりに多く

42. Kono yowa o / Kora no nemuri mo / Hakobitsutsu
Deigo sakitsugu shima / Kaeri kinu
この夜半を子らの眠りも運びつつデイゴ咲きつぐ島還り来ぬ

43. Saniwabe ni / Natsu murakusa no / Kaori tachi
Hoshi yawarakani / Ko no me ni ochinu
さ庭べに夏むらくさの香りたち星やはらかに子の目におちぬ

44. Tamayura ni / Furuki yo no hi no / Iro yurete
Ochikochi no nobe / Yakarete aran
たまゆらに古き世の火の色揺れてをちこちの野辺焼かれてあらむ

45. Eda hosomi / Kiburi yasashiku / Kohigan no
Haru hitotoki o / Hana tsukeni keri
枝細み木ぶりやさしく小彼岸の春ひと時を花つけにけり

46. Honokani mo / Yure nagare kuru / Gaku no ne ari
Uta-mai no hitora / Hagemite aran
ほのかにも揺れ流れ来る楽の音あり歌舞の人らはげみてあらむ

47. Iku nemuri / Sugoshishi Harugo / Sudenishite
Tōru shirosa ni / Ito haki somenu
いく眠り過ごしし春蚕すでにして透る白さに糸吐き初めぬ

48. Aogitsutsu / Hana erami ishi / Kobushi no ki no
Eda sagari kinu / Kimi ni motarete
仰ぎつつ花えらみゐし辛夷の木の枝さがりきぬ君に持たれて

49. Kotonareru / Hankyū ni areba / Yuku aki to
Minatsuki no niwa ni / Hayaki shimo oku
異なれる半球にあれば行く秋と水無月の庭に早き霜おく

50. Asakaze ni / Mukaite hashiru / Shinshō no
Miwa takarakani / Kyoka o kazashite
朝風に向かひて走る身障の身は高らかに炬火をかざして

51. Sazanka no / Sakeru komichi no / Ochibataki
    Dōyō to seshi / Hito no ima naku
    山茶花の咲ける小道の落葉焚き童謡とせし人の今亡く

52. Fuyuzora o / Ginga wa chichi to / Nagareite
    Midorigo kimi wa / Nemuri imashiken
    冬空を銀河は乳と流れゐてみどりご君は眠りいましけむ

53. Jōan ni / Utsuri tamaite / Yasurakeku
    Ake somururan / Asa to shinoinu
    浄闇に遷り給ひてやすらけく明けそむるらむ朝としのひぬ

54. Omoi egaku / Koganei no sato / Mugi no ho yure
    Shōnen no hi no / Kimi tachitamau
    思ひゑがく小金井の里麦の穂揺れ少年の日の君立ち給ふ

55. Natsu wakaki / Shirakaba kodachi / Hadarenasu
    Kage fumi kora no / Tsugitsugi ni yuku
    夏稚き白樺木立はだれなす影ふみ子らのつぎつぎに行く

56. Kakojimo no / Tada hitorigo o / Sasageshito
    Gokokujinja ni / Kataru haha wamo
    鹿子じものただ一人子を捧げしと護国神社に語る母はも

57. Miwa no sato / Sai no watari ni / Kyō mo kamo
    Hana shizumesu to / Matsurite aran
    三輪の里狭井のわたりに今日もかも花鎮めすと祭りてあらむ

58. Adokenaki / Nobe no matsuri ka / Osanara no
    Ojizō-sama ni / Furete hana maku
    あどけなき野辺の祭か幼らのお地蔵さまに触れて花播く

59. Izukata no / Minato ni irishi / Fune naran
    Muteki hibiki ki / Asage no heya ni
    いづ方の港に入りし船ならむ霧笛響き来朝餉の室に

60. Sora ni uku / Yamaararagi no / Katazaki o
    Tsuki honoyakani / Terashite yamazu
    空に浮くやまあららぎの片咲きを月ほのやかに照らしてやまず

61. Shiokaze ni / Tachite honami no / Kuzureyuku
    Sama mite arishi / Ryōyō no hibi
    汐風に立ちて秀波の崩れゆくさま見てありし療養の日日

62. Ikusa uma ni / Sodatsu kouma no / Uta arite
    Osanaki hi kuni wa / Tatakaite iki
    いくさ馬に育つ仔馬の歌ありて幼なき日国は戦ひてゐき

63. Wakuraba no / Chiri shiku naka ni / Miidashishi
    Kigisu no hane o / Ko wa pen to suru
    わくらばの散り敷く中に見いだししきぎすの羽を子はペンとする

64. Itamitsutsu / Nao yasashikumo / Hitora sumu
    Yūna saku shima no / Saka nobori yuku
    いたみつつなほ優しくも人ら住むゆうな咲く島の坂のぼりゆく

65. Buri-okoshi / Hokuriku no sora / Toyomoshite
    Oki ni ideyuku / Funabitora naran
    鰤起し北陸の空とよもして沖に出でゆく船人らならむ

66. Utsushi-e no / Toki wa haru kamo / Osana ware o
    Idaku tarachineno / Haha wakakarishi
    うつし絵の時は春かも幼な我を抱くたらちねの母若かりし

67. Utsukushiki / Koe ni katareri / Meshiitsutsu
    Koto hiku hito no / Tēpu no tayori
    美しき声に語れり盲ひつつ琴ひく人のテープの便り

68. Sora ni koru / Inori no gotoku / Hitohira no
    Shirakumo wa tō no / Ue ni ukaberi
    空に凝る祈りの如く一ひらの白雲は塔の上に浮かべり

69. Mitsukai no / Tabi no mitomo to / Kyō wa tou
Ki naru hana sakaru / Adoria no kishi
み使ひの旅のみ伴と今日は訪ふ黄なる花さかるアドリアの岸

70. Fuyumoya no / Naka o shizukani / Sakunaran
Saga no chaen no / Shiroki hana tatsu
冬靄の中を静かに咲くならむ佐賀の茶園の白き花顕つ

71. Misaki mina / Umi terasan to / Tomoru toki
Yumi nashite akaru / Kono kuni naran
岬みな海照らさむと点るとき弓なして明かるこの国ならむ

72. Yūmado o / Tozasan hima o / Tatazumite
Mikazuki no kage ni / Shibaraku hitaru
夕窓を閉ざさむひまを佇みて若月のかげにしばらくひたる

73. Sono no hate ni / Ōshimazakura / Tou to iu
Ko ni kasanegi no / Kinu o motasenu
園の果てに大島桜訪ふといふ子に重ね着の衣をもたせぬ

74. Koinobori / Osameshi nochi no / Yūgure o
Hitori asobi no / Yaguruma meguru
鯉のぼり納めしのちの夕暮をひとり遊びの矢車めぐる

75. Kuzu no hana / Hakage ni sakite / Natsu takuru
Hibi koyarimasu / Hahamiya ietamae
くずの花葉かげに咲きて夏たくる日日臥ります母宮癒え給へ

76. Osana wako no / Yorokobeba mata / Shikirinimo
Kizahashi uchite / Shii no mi ochikuru
幼な吾子の喜べば又しきりにもきざはし打ちて椎の実落ち来る

77. Ko ni tsugenu / Kanashimi mo aran o / Hahasoha no
Haha sugayakani / Oi tamai keri
子に告げぬ哀しみもあらむを柞葉の母清やかに老い給ひけり

184

78. Rāgeru ni / Kikoku no shirase / Matsu haru no
    Sawarabi wa shida ni / Narite sugishito
    ラーゲルに帰国のしらせ待つ春の早蕨は羊歯になりて過ぎしと

79. Furanki yori / Ideshi hiyokora / Hakonuchi no
    Denkyū no nukumori ni / Mi o yose nemuru
    孵卵器より出しひよこら箱ぬちの電球の温もりに身を寄せ眠る

80. Misora yori / Ima zo mitamae / Horimashishi
    Nihon rettō ni / Sakura sakitsugu
    み空より今ぞ見給へ欲りましし日本列島に桜咲き継ぐ

81. Shiratori mo / Karigane mo mata / Tabidachite
    Ōyashimaguni / Haru towa nareri
    白鳥も雁がねもまた旅立ちておほやしまぐに春とはなれり

82. Ike no mo ni / Yutani utsureru / Samidori no
    Kasukani yurete / Medakara yukinu
    池の面に豊に映れるさみどりのかすかに揺れて目高ら行きぬ

83. Machiishi kaze / Tachisomeshiran / Wakakira no
    Ayatsuru yotto / Niwakani hayashi
    待ちゐし風立ちそめしらむ若きらのあやつるヨツトにはかに速し

84. Umi no be no / Yōmanjō o / Ashita tou
    Yoshikiri no naku / Ashihara o kite
    湖の辺の養鰻場を朝訪ふよしきりの鳴く芦原を来て

85. Kanohi toishi / Akita no sato no / Oi no ie
    Tatsuki ikanaran / Yuki-gakoi no uchi
    かの日訪ひし秋田の里の老の家たつきいかならむ雪がこひのうち

86. Tabi iwau to / Maikoshi oka no / Misasagi ni
    Hana sawani motsu / Misakaki sasagu
    旅斎ふと参来し丘のみささぎに花さはに持つみ榊捧ぐ

185

87. Kozo no hoshi / Yadoseru sora ni / Toshi akete
    Saitansai ni / Kimi idetamau

去年の星宿せる空に年明けて歳旦祭に君いでたまふ

88. Kono toshi mo / Tsuyukeku sakan / Benibana to
    Tenohira ni shiroki / Tane o miteori

この年も露けく咲かむ紅花と掌に白き種を見てをり

89. Kumo mo naku / Myōjō no hikari / Sayakanaru
    Kono akatoki no / Sono no shizukesa

雲もなく明星の光さやかなるこのあかときの園の静けさ

90. Nasu no no no / Numachi ni sakuo / Hitsuji-gusa to
    Oshie tamaiki / Kano hi kooshimo

那須の野の沼地に咲くを未草と教へ給ひきかの日恋ほしも

91. Otome naru / Hitohi bokin ni / Tachishi hi no
    Ekimae no hizashi / Omoi dasaruru

をとめなるひと日募金に立ちし日の駅前の日ざし思ひださるる

92. Netsudei no / Umeshi Temmei no / Mura no ato
    Horu hitomure ni / Wako mo majireru

熱泥の埋めし天明の村のあと掘る人群に吾子もまじれる

93. Niiname no / Mimatsuri hatete / Kaerimasu
    Kimi no mikoromo / Yaki hiebieshi

新嘗のみ祭果てて還ります君のみ衣夜気冷えびえし

94. Kono toshi mo / Kaku kureyukuka / Kaidō ni
    Kyūseigun no / Jizennabe miyu

この年もかく暮れゆくか街道に救世軍の慈善鍋見ゆ

95. Kaze fukeba / Osanaki wako o / Tamayurani
    Akaruku hedatsu / Sakura-fubuki wa

風ふけば幼なき吾子を玉ゆらに明るくへだつ桜ふぶきは

96. Inochi ete kano kisaragi no / yūbe shimo kono yo ni
areshi / midorigo no hatatose o hete / ima koko ni ui
ni kōburu / asagi naru warawa no fuku ni / warawa
kamuru kūchōkokusaku / sono kazashi tokihanatarete /
aratanaru kuroki kagafuri / itadaki ni shikatoshi okare /
shiroki kakeo kamuri o kudari / wakaki hoho
tsutaitsutaite / agito no shita kataku musubare / sono
shiroki kakeo no amari / oto sayani sayani tatarenu

Hatatose o sugishi hi to nashi / osanabi o kako to wa
nashite / kokoro tadani kiyorani akaku / kono hi
yori tadori ayuman / mioya mina ayumi tamaishi /
masugunaru ōkinaru michi / seinen no miko to shi
ikuru / kono michi ni ima shi tatasu wako / waya

Hanka

Oto sayani / kakeo kirareshi / ko no tateba / harokeku
tōshi / kano kisaragi wa

いのち得てかの如月の　夕しもこの世に生れし　みどりごの二十年を
経て　今ここに初に冠る　浅黄なる童の服に　童かむる空頂黒幘
そのかざし解き放たれて　新たなる黒き冠　頂にしかとし置かれ
白き懸緒かむりを降り　若き頬伝ひつたひて　顎の下堅く結ばれ
その白き懸緒の余　音さやにさやに絶たれぬ

はたとせを過ぎし日となし　幼日を過去とは為して　心ただに清らに
明かく　この日よりたどり歩まむ　御祖みな歩み給ひし　真直なる
大きなる道　成年の皇子とし生くる　この道に今し立たす吾子　はや

反　歌
音さやに懸緒截られし子の立てばはろけく遠しかの如月は

97. Harukusa no / Hatsuhatsu izuru / Dote no sama
　　Minto shundei no / Michi ayumi yuku
春草のはつはつ出づる土手のさま見むと春泥の道あゆみゆく

187

98. Mihoribe no / Hosō no michi no / Akarukini
    Hana chiri shikite / Wakaki eji tatsu
    み堀辺の舗装の道の明かるきに花散り敷きて若き衛士立つ

99. Kai torite / Asobishi higata / Toshi o hete
    Waga omoide no / Naka ni hirogaru
    貝採りて遊びし干潟年を経てわが思ひ出の中にひろがる

100. Mugi no ho no / Sukoyakani nobi / Kono toshi mo
    Shimo no wakare no / Koro to naritari
    麦の穂のすこやかに伸びこの年も霜の別れの頃となりたり

101. Kuroku ureshi / Kuwa no mi ware no / Te ni okite
    Sokai no hibi o / Kimi wa katarasu
    くろく熟れし桑の実われの手に置きて疎開の日日を君は語らす

102. Nagaki yo no / Manabi susumu wa / Tanoshitozo
    Norishi ko no kotoba / Idakite inuru
    長き夜の学び進むは楽しとぞ宣りし子の言葉抱きて寝ぬる

103. Yowa no mizu / Oyobini shimite / Araitaru
    Kono suzuri nagaku / Tsukai kitarishi
    夜半の水およびに凍みて洗ひたるこの硯長く使ひ来りし

104. Hiiragi no / Oishi hitoki wa / Toge no naki
    Zen'en no ha to / Naritaru aware
    柊の老いし一木は刺のなき全縁の葉となりたるあはれ

105. Michinoku mo / Tsukushi no hate mo / Narimashinu
    Michi katakarishi / Kano miyo ni shite
    みちのくも筑紫の果ても成りましぬ道難かりしかの御代にして

106. Waga kimi no / Mikuruma ni sou / Akikawa no
    Seoto o kiyomi / Tomonaware yuku
    わが君のみ車にそふ秋川の瀬音を清みともなはれゆく

188

107. Yamutoshi mo / Naku furitsuzuku / Ame no naka
Kosamuki sono ni / Ume no mi o toru
やむとしもۤなく降り続く雨のۣなか小寒き園に梅の実を採る

108. Unohana no / Hanaakari suru / Yūgure ni
Mita no sanae o / Omoitsutsu yuku
卯の花の花明かりする夕暮れに御田の早苗を想ひつつゆく

109. Aki-higan / Yōyaku chikaku / Shirakumo no
Hitotsu ukaberu / Yama no shizukesa
秋彼岸やうやく近く白雲の一つ浮かべる山の静けさ

110. Itsushika ni / Hamura o koete / Chichiiro no
Yatsude no hana no / Tama totonoeru
いつしかに葉群を越えて乳色の八つ手の花の球ととのへる

111. Hashi hitotsu / Watari kitareba / Sangatsu no
Hikari ni miyuru / Kaijō no toshi
橋ひとつ渡り来たれば三月のひかりに見ゆる海上の都市

112. Ume no ka o / Fufumu kaze ari / Koshi oka no
Yaya samuku shite / Tsukushi wa imada
梅の香をふふむ風あり来し丘のやや寒くして土筆はいまだ

113. Kōkyo hōshi no / Hitora no iishi / Sukagawa no
Sono no botan o / Yowa ni omoeru
皇居奉仕の人らの言ひし須賀川の園の牡丹を夜半に想へる

114. Mitezukara / Uetamaikeru / Sanaeda no
Kotoshi no minori / Yutakani aran
みてづから植ゑ給ひける早苗田の今年の実り豊かにあらむ

115. Ame yamite / Niwakani atsuki / Hi no saseba
Totonoe okishi / Usumono ureshi
雨止みてにはかに暑き日の射せばととのへ置きし羅うれし

116. Kono tsuki wa / Wako no are tsuki / Yomosugara
Kikishi kogarashi no / Oto o wasurezu
この月は吾子の生れ月夜もすがら聞きし木枯の音を忘れず

117. Shihōi o / Nami ni yomitsutsu / Kogite koshi
Yappu no shima no / Hito wasurarezu
四方位を波に読みつつ漕ぎて来しヤップの島の人忘られず

118. Hi o machite / Hoshi no hitotsu to / Narite tobu
Roketto miori / Shima kaze no naka
日を待ちて星の一つとなりてとぶロケット見をり島風のなか

119. Hitosuji ni / Yama medeshi hito / Towa ni nemuru
Nepāru no yama / Kyō mo fubukuka
ひとすぢに山愛でし人永遠に眠るネパールの山今日も吹雪くか

120. Sakuramochi / Sono kaori yoku / Tsutsumi iru
Yawarakaki ha mo / Tomoni hami keri
さくらもちその香りよく包みゐる柔らかき葉も共にはみけり

121. Onozukara / Take takakushite / Sugasugashi
Wakatake majiru / Kono takamura wa
おのづから丈高くしてすがすがし若竹まじるこのたかむらは

122. Miteue no / Sugi o idakite / Ranjō wa
Midori no mori to / Narite sakayuru
み手植ゑの杉を抱きて頼成は緑の森となりて栄ゆる

123. Hyōshōjō / Ukuru sono te wa / Toshitsuki o
Yamayama no midori / Hagukumite koshi
表彰状受くるその手は年月を山やまの緑はぐくみて来し

124. Kakaru yoi / Ware wa konomu to / Iu wako no
Mami yasashimite / Higurashi o kiku
かかる宵われは好むといふ吾娘のまみ優しみて蜩をきく

190

125. Totsukuni ni / Wako hanare sumu / Kono toshi no
      Yoru no shizukesa / Nagaku omowan
    外国に吾子離れすむこの年の夜のしづけさ長くおもはむ

126. Kokoyashi no / Midori no ue ni / Ōinaru
      Afurika no sora / Ashita moe somu
    ココ椰子の緑の上に大いなるアフリカの空あした燃えそむ

127. Kodomora no / Koe kikoe kite / Hiroba naru
      Funsui no hono / Takaku tatsu miyu
    子供らの声きこえ来て広場なる噴水のほの高く立つ見ゆ

128. Satsuma naru / Kiire no saka o / Nobori kite
      Nemu no hana mishi / Natsu no hi omou
    薩摩なる喜入の坂を登り来て合歓の花見し夏の日想ふ

129. Matsumushi no / Koe ni majirite / Yoru osoku
      Ko no hiku naran / Gitā no oto su
    松虫の声にまじりて夜遅く子の弾くならむギターの音す

130. Toite koshi / Mura wa kosumosu no / Saki sakari
      Mahiru no sora ni / Iwashigumo uku
    訪ひて来し村はコスモスの咲き盛り真昼の空に鰯雲浮く

131. Osanagami / Nadeyarishi hi mo / Tōkushite
      Otome sabitsutsu / Ko wa tabidachinu
    幼な髪なでやりし日も遠くしてをとめさびつつ子は旅立ちぬ

132. Mitomo seru / Tabiji no shasō / Akarumite
      'Hana ippai' no / Machi o sugiyuku
    み伴せる旅路の車窓明かるみて「花一杯」の町を過ぎゆく

133. Tabishi koshi / Arubion no haru / Asaku shite
      Hana hatsukanari / Gakuto no tsuchi ni
    旅し来し英国の春浅くして花はつかなり学都の土に

134. Umikaze o / Motome tabiyuku / Wakakira o
Hansen wa matsu / Tsuki no minato ni
うみ風を求め旅行く若きらを帆船は待つ月の港に

135. Haru no hi no / Yururu oima ni / Kono yoi o
Hihina no gotoku / Kimi mo imasan
春の灯のゆるる御居間にこの宵をひひなの如く君もいまさむ

136. Inazuma to / Raimei no ma o / Kazoetsutsu
Hina ni osanaku / Arishi hibi wamo
稲妻と雷鳴の間をかぞへつつ鄙に幼くありし日日はも

137. Mokusei no / Hana sakini keri / Kono toshi no
Tōkyō no sora / Sayakani sumite
木犀の花咲きにけりこの年の東京の空さやかに澄みて

138. Mado ni sasu / Yūbae akaku / To no mo naru
No ni fuyugare no / Tsuyoki kaze fuku
窓にさす夕映え赤く外の面なる野に冬枯れの強き風ふく

139. Sasu koete / Ohōtsuku no umi / Nozomitari
Saroma no mizu ni / Chigyo o hanachite
砂州越えてオホーツクの海望みたり佐呂間の水に稚魚を放ちて

140. Kono toshi no / Kono yoki haru no / Akaki momo
Kimi miyowai o / Kasane tamaeri
この年のこのよき春の紅き桃君みよはひを重ね給へり

STAFF

Editors: Marie Philomène and Masako Saito

Consultants: Rikutaro Fukuda
Peter Milward
Kristen Deming

Collaborators in translation:

Poems by Emperor Akihito

Marie Philomène
Michiko Wada
Toshimi Horiuchi
Tomiko Hirata
Satoko Yoshino
Harumi Sugiyama
Osamu Yoshihara

Poems by Empress Michiko

Masako Saito
Mutsumi Miyamoto
Teruko Craig
Yuki Yamada
Marie Philomène
Keiko Kikuchi
Yumiko Terasaka

The "weathermark" identifies this book as a production of Tanko-Weatherhill, Inc., publishers of fine books on Asia and the Pacific. General supervision: Yoshiharu Naya. Typography: Miriam F. Yamaguchi. Book design: Miriam F. Yamaguchi and Norio Ishiguro. Production supervision: Mitsuo Okado. Composition, engraving, printing, and binding: Dai Nippon Printing Co., Ltd., Tokyo. Paper specially manufactured for this book by Hokuetsu Paper Mills Limited, Tokyo. Typeface used is Monotype Bembo.